THE GLORY OF HIS DAY

Have we forgotten God's promise
of great blessing for mankind?

John Dudley Aldworth

THE GLORY OF HIS DAY

Copyright © 2022 John Dudley Aldworth

First edition published January 2022.

The moral right of the author to full ownership of the copyright of 'The Glory of His Day' has been asserted. All rights are reserved. The book may not be reproduced in part or whole without prior written permission from the publisher. However, extracts for the purpose of Bible study, sermons, and reviews in magazines, newspapers, radio and television, and quotations in other books are allowed.

Publisher: **Truthful History Publications**
Email: john.aldworth@hotmail.com

Cover Photo: NASA, Public Domain
Cover Design by: Jan Kaluza http://jankaluza.net/homepg.php
Prepared for publication by: WordWyze Publishing Ltd http://wordwyze.nz

Most Scriptures are from the Authorised King James Version, Public Domain.

Scripture quotations marked (AMP) taken from the Amplified Bible (AMP), Copyright © 2015 by The Lockman Foundation. Used by permission, www.lockman.org.

Scripture quotations marked (ASV) are taken from the American Standard Version Bible (Public Domain).

Scripture quotations marked (NASB) taken from the New American Standard Bible® (NASB), copyright© 1960, 1962, 1963, 1968, 1971, 1972, 1973, 1975, 1977, 1995 by the Lockman Foundation. Used by permission, www.lockman.org.

Scripture quotations marked (NEB) taken from New English Bible® Oxford University Press and Cambridge University Press 1961, 1970. Used by permission.

Scripture quotations marked (NIV) taken from The Holy Bible, New International Version® (NIV®) Copyright© 1973, 1978, 1984, 2011 by Biblica, Inc.® Used by permission. www.biblica.com.

Scripture references marked (NKJV) are from the New King James Version. Copyright © 1982 by Thomas Nelson, Inc. Used by permission. All rights reserved.

A catalogue record for this book is available from the National Library of New Zealand.

Paperback ISBN: 978-0-473-62478-1

Contents

PREFACE GOD'S GREATEST BLESSING YET iv
FOREWORD vi
WHY THIS BOOK? 8
Chapter One - ARE WE READY FOR THE LORD'S BLAZE OF GLORY? 13
Chapter Two - ARE WE STILL LOOKING FOR HIS APPEARING? 23
Chapter Three - IS THERE A CURE FOR OUR COMPLAINT? 31
Chapter Four - ENLIGHTENMENT IN THE DAY OF CHRIST 37
Chapter Five - THE DAY OF MAN AND THE DAY OF CHRIST 45
Chapter Six - TWO INTO ONE WON'T GO 53
Chapter Seven - THE DAY OF CHRIST AND OUR SALVATION 57
Chapter Eight - CAN WE FEEL GOD? 65
Chapter Nine - A DIRECT EXPERIENCE OF HIS GLORY 71
Chapter Ten - EMPOWERED BY HIS GLORY NOW 77
Chapter Eleven - IS THE TABERNACLE OF DAVID A KEY? 85
Chapter Twelve - THE FINGER OF GOD 95
Chapter Thirteen - GENTILE BLESSINGS IN THE DAY OF CHRIST 101
Chapter Fourteen - THE APPOINTED DAY OF JUDGEMENT 125
Chapter Fifteen - IS IT HIS REVELATION OR HIS COMING? 131
Chapter Sixteen - THE GLORY TO FOLLOW 135
Chapter Seventeen - WAS JESUS MADE SICK FOR US? 141
Chapter Eighteen - IS JESUS JUST A MAN? 153
Chapter Nineteen - PASSPORT TO GLORY 159
Chapter Twenty - SO WHAT SHOULD WE DO? 163
APPENDIX - SATAN'S GREAT TIME HOAX 169
APPENDIX - TIMING – THE SECRET OF THE KINGDOM PARABLES 179
APPENDIX - THE SEED THAT GROWS BY ITSELF 187

PREFACE
GOD'S GREATEST BLESSING YET

What lies ahead both for the world and those who trust Jesus? Will the Lord return tomorrow in flaming fire to destroy those who refuse to believe his gospel (2 Thess. 1:8)? Or will He instead blaze forth his glory to bring his greatest blessings thus far upon the earth and mankind (Titus 2:13 and Isa. 11:9)?

Many believe the 'rapture' is next on God's agenda. They hold there will follow the 'great tribulation', the 'second coming' and the *'day of the Lord'* in which God will wreak vengeance and death on those 'left behind' because they refuse to heed Him. But stand by for a shock. That order of events is not what the apostles taught.

They assert that instead God's next big move will be one of glory and restoration. Christ will blaze out his glory in a dazzling display (Titus 2:13) *'and all flesh shall see it together for the Lord hath spoken'* (Isa. 40:5). Prophecy says He will then take over government of the world and restore mankind and the earth to what they were before the Flood, recreating a world of righteousness, peace and plenty.

When on earth, Jesus called this wonderful age *'the world to come'*. Paul seven times describes it as the *'day of Christ'* (1 Cor. 1:8, etc.), sharply distinguishing it from the *'day of the Lord'* (I Thess. 5:2*)* which, I submit, in God's plan of the ages, comes later. Peter proclaimed the preceding, world-changing eon of glory as *'the times of restitution of all things spoken by the prophets since the world began'* (Acts 3:21).

The prophets of old say this glorious day will see sickness and poverty banished, sin rebuked and evil vanquished. Justice and equity will prevail and the earth will be restored to its originally created splendour. Curses will be lifted and the spiritual powers of darkness seized and jailed. Best of all, God's glory will fill all the earth (Num. 14:21)

In nearly 50 years as a Christian, I have never heard a church sermon preached on this soon-to-be wonderful day. But in this book, you can learn about this era which will see God bring greatest blessing since Adam sinned in the Garden of Eden, and perhaps even receive your own foretaste of this glory to come.

FOREWORD

Today it is little known and scarcely mentioned but once the *'day of Jesus Christ'*, prophesied repeatedly in Paul's epistles, was considered of supreme importance. In fact, two of the greatest Bible expositors ever held that it was the 'day of his **appearing**' and as such a separate event preceding the Lord's *parousia*, his return to earth. It would be a day in which Christ would triumph and finalise every believer's salvation.

Sadly, little or no explanation of just what the *'day of Christ'* will be found in more modern Bible commentaries. Nor does it find treatment as an amazing era in its own right in latter-day schemes of interpreting biblically prophesied future events.

Yet, the highly respected theologian and much-cited Bible commentator, Matthew Henry (1622-1714), saw this day as vital to the completion of our salvation. He wrote:

> 'The work of grace will never be perfected till the day of Jesus Christ, the day of his appearance. But we may always be confident God will perform his good work, in every soul wherein he has really begun it by regeneration; though we must not trust in outward appearances, nor in anything but a new creation to holiness'.

Furthermore, that great Bible scholar and prolific commentator Albert Barnes (1798-1870) in his *Notes on the Bible*: comments that the day of Jesus Christ is:

> 'The day when Christ shall so manifest himself as to be the great attractive object, or the day when he shall

appear to glorify himself, so that it may be said emphatically to be his day. It will be the day of his triumph and glory.'

For the record, Albert Barnes' exegetical *'Notes'* were considered required reading, and formed the basis of much preaching, by John Wesley, George Whitefield and Charles Haddon Spurgeon. So, his understanding of the *'day of Christ'* should be foundational in our evangelical inheritance.

So, why is it widely ignored among Bible teachers of today? Could it be the overlooked but important Bible key to truly understanding what God will do next?

WHY THIS BOOK?

God, I believe, has a purpose for every person born. Especially those He causes to be born again. Many, of course, fail to take up their God-given destiny. Others seek to serve the Lord and struggle and suffer to do so. I fall into the latter category.

Now in my autumn, God is knitting together the ragged tapestry of my years to meld knowledge from Bible study with the many tangible spiritual blessings He has given me. Such fusion now bridges the gulf which for years separated the two.

Let me explain: Some fifty years ago I was saved when God in a blaze of glory showed me He was real. (A later chapter will tell more of the story). This filled me with hunger for his word and within weeks of being baptised I bought a hefty reference Bible. Studying scripture became a daily habit.

But there were also miracles and I received words of knowledge, prophecies and revelations from the Lord as I later shared his truth as an evangelist, pastor and Bible teacher. Problem was, I had yet to learn to clearly distinguish experiences truly of the Spirit from those of the flesh, of the mind, will and emotions. When real evil broke out both in church and in my family, I wrongly concluded Pentecostal experience was to blame and turned my back on it.

There followed years in the wilderness but eventually God led me back to Himself through an intense experience of grace as taught from the Word. I learned that we are now in the dispensation of the grace of God (Eph. 3:2) and that the good news today is the gospel of the grace of God in which we are not under the law.

However, this 'dispensationalism' came with a catch. By over zealously *'rightly dividing the word of truth'* (2 Tim. 2:15) proponents of this system wrongly taught that most miracles and overt 'signs and wonders' of the Holy Ghost came to a halt at the end of the book of Acts. Those that continued, they said, were mainly bogus.

I fell for this line of thinking but in time learned it is not true. Our God and Saviour Jesus Christ is *'the same yesterday, today and forever'* (Heb. 13:8). Granted, there are new teachings such as reconciliation of the world (1 John 2:2), brought about by grace and the revelation of the mystery (Rom. 16:25).

But these all result from the Lord's tremendous achievements in his death, burial, resurrection and ascension. Known unto God all along, they have been imparted in a progressive series of revelations given to the apostles and recorded in their letters. And those revelations often come with physically real, tangible experiences in the Holy Spirit.

Suffice to say that God had to show me that a diet of strenuously studying the Word without 'spiritual fireworks' from the Holy Ghost was not enough. He did so by drawing the Bible study fellowship I taught to a close and leaving my wife and I seeking healing for the stroke she suffered.

Enter a full-on Pentecostal neighbour who insisted we seek a miracle for Naomi's recovery at a church which conducted healing meetings. She refused to agree such manifestations had ceased at the end of Acts and persisted in her invitations. After some months of this we gave in and went. It was at my second attendance that a word of prophecy was directed at me and when prayed for I was knocked to the floor in a blaze of glory. It took that to convince me afresh that God's power and presence are forever real.

Now, forgive me if, at first glance, the message in this book is not quite your cup of tea. I freely admit it does not spring from the mould of commonly held ideas about God, what He is doing now, and what comes next. However, I assure you it stems from nearly half a century of Bible study and seeking and being radically changed by the Lord. Add to the mix years spent as an investigative journalist, sub-editor and editor – skills I applied to studying His Word, the Bible.

The outcome is a message I believe will touch your heart as it has indeed touched mine. Already the Lord is speaking it worldwide to all who will listen to what He really has to say. The truth comes, sometimes in words hard to be uttered, to all who love Him.

You see, as a journalist I long ago learned to seek the facts beneath the bland, outward appearance of political statements, the euphemistic assurances of big business and the half-truths of those who resort to sin and lies to justify their position.

And to further my understanding, God, over the years, has exposed me to the *'many winds of doctrine'* (Eph. 4:14) blowing about in Christian circles. Not to be persuaded by them but to rise above them and go beyond them to find from scripture answers to the many questions all seekers after God's truth have. Answers that only the Spirit of Christ within us can reveal and confirm according to his written word.

Among the important lessons learned in this quest were the following:

1. One must be led by the Spirit and get understanding of truth direct from God Himself, not just pick it up second-hand from the biblical interpretations of others. That is to say, one must be personally *'...taught by Jesus...just as the truth is in Jesus'* (Eph. 4:21).

2. Bible study must be holistic. That is, it must be based, not on partial understanding, but on the whole truth as presented in scripture. Didn't Jesus call two disciples he met on the Emmaus road *'fools'* because they were *'…slow of heart to believe **all** that the prophets have spoken'?* (Luke 24:25). Not some of it but all of it. So, one should not omit some things to create a simpler picture, which in the end may prove wrong. Recently, a minister jokingly suggested my citing the *'day of Christ'* (1 Cor. 1:8, 5:5; Phil. 1:6, 2:16 and other scriptures) as the next big event on God's calendar, might be 'heresy'. Well, if truth spoken by God at the start of time, reiterated by his prophets down the ages, taught as essential truth by Jesus, and repeated by the apostles in their writings, be heresy, then I plead guilty.
3. Such truth as is discovered must also be God's saving message for the time in which we live. Not just to reach the lost as individuals but also to save and change for the better whole families, communities at large, nations, indeed the whole world. Because that is what a whole study of scripture demands.
4. An acid test of such truth is whether it comes with the anointing of the Holy Spirit to soften hearts and change minds to surrender to God's will, for the teaching must be understood in love. To sum up, in addition to being governed by the Word of God in scripture, I have learned that in all things I must be led by the Spirit of God.

Chapter One -
ARE WE READY FOR THE LORD'S BLAZE OF GLORY?

Can we see the Lord's glory in this lifetime, before we die? Will Jesus step in to save our world before we destroy it? Can the life of heaven be manifested on earth indeed to restore our home to its pre-Flood pristine beauty? Surprisingly, the biblical answer to each of these questions seems to be a resounding 'Yes'.

Because, for one thing, Jesus Himself prayed both for us and for the world to see his glory (John 17:24). That is, the glory the Father gave Him before the world began when through the devil's temptation and man's sin things went wrong. I strongly believe God is about to fulfil his long-standing promise to put everything right, banishing sin and sickness, lifting the curse and restoring earth to its original beauty. And, in terms of glory, until that happens it's appropriate to say we 'ain't seen nothing yet'.

For, the shining forth of his glory at his **appearing** - Greek: *epiphanea:* a blazing out of light (Titus 2:13) - will bring in a whole new, and much better, age. This will be Christ's day, and my conviction is that God has it as the very next date on his prophetic calendar. What's more, I believe that even now right now we can get a foretaste of that glory before it comes in its fullness. After all, didn't the Apostle Peter say nearly 2,000 years ago that he was even then a partaker of *'the glory that should be revealed'* (2 Pet. 5:1). And if him then, why not us now? Detail on that and much else later.

First though, let's consider why the Lord should step in to save His world right now. Because that is what we should be asking and expecting Him to do. Fact is the world is so full of hate, fear and evil it's a miracle God wants to save it at all. But He does. And, be sure of this, save it He will. Didn't Jesus say He came *'not to judge the world but to save the world'* (John 12:47)? Didn't the Samaritans hail Him as *'the Saviour of the world'* (John 4:4:42)? Doesn't the Apostle John testify in 1 John 4:14 that *'the Father sent the Son to be the Saviour of the world'*?

Right now, for we Christians there perhaps has never been a time when the manifestation of Christ's glory has been needed more. As ones saved by his grace, cleansed by His blood, filled with his Spirit and experiencing his presence, we need to ask ourselves why we are not experiencing a greater measure of the light of his glory.

Surely, a fresh spark of his light and life is needed to renew fire in the heart of the many who are faltering in the faith. And a glimpse of the Lord Jesus Christ's glory would bring real hope to the many believers around the world today suffering and dying for his name's sake.

And, please note, it was much more than a glimpse - it was a blazing revelation - of the Lord's glory that was seen by the Lord's apostles during their lifetime. Good reason then, to believe that the Lord can likewise reveal Himself in dazzling light to each one of us in our here and now.

Without doubt such light is desperately needed in the church where today doors are closing as numbers dwindle. And the Body of Christ as a whole seems sadly ineffective. Her voice is not heard in the street, nor in the counsels of the world. Many pastors have become dumb dogs afraid to bark publicly for fear of the consequences. This, even when lawmakers enact measures which defy God and His truth and deny us our freedom.

No wonder then, as our world plunges deeper into crisis, it seems few are being saved. Certainly, the gospel has ample power to save but what price that when few want to listen? And, as Jesus said, labourers for the harvest are few. Today then, the church is in dire need of seeing afresh the glory of the Lord.

As to the world, woe to it, for calamities are an everyday occurrence now. No sooner does one disaster overwhelm part of the earth than another elsewhere follows in its wake. In the West the safe and prosperous post-war years are vanishing like smoke before the wind. None can be sure what tomorrow will bring. And desperation, war, hunger, disease, and famine continue to stalk much of the rest of the world.

For all these ills, God's answer is, as it has always been, the shining forth of his glory through his Son Jesus Christ. And the good news is that the Lord has promised to so **appear** in person to shine forth his glory to all who will believe and look for it, both now in our lifetime and also in his wonderful new *'world to come'* (see Matt. 12:32, Mark 10:30, Luke 18:30, Heb. 2:5, 6:5).

By the way, it's important to realise this wonderful new world of righteousness, peace and everlasting life takes place on earth, not in heaven. Doesn't the Lord's Prayer say: *'Thy kingdom come …on* **earth***'?* At least it did when I last read it. And rightly read there is nothing in the Bible to say that the kingdom cannot come right this very minute. More on that later.

A message for our time?

So, is there a message God has for his people in this crucial hour? Is there a doctrine, a portion of scripture we have overlooked that God would quicken to us? Could it be that God has allowed such truth to be hidden until now so that it can be brought to light in today's crisis hour when, arguably, it is most needed? I firmly believe that is so.

Certainly, we as believers cannot go on doing what we have always done, repeating that which failed to work yesterday, expecting that somehow it will work today. And how can Christians unsure of their own salvation in practical terms *'hold forth the word of life'* to others (Phil. 2:16)? To society at large the church has become an anachronism; it is not influencing the world; rather the world is reshaping the church in its own image. God needs to step in and stop the rot and, in my view, if we will believe it, He will.

To go on having a small taste of the Lord's presence on Sunday morning (but long gone by Monday) will not suffice. Precious as such moments are they will not bring about the huge change required to see *'all the earth filled with the glory of the Lord'* (Num. 14:21). Can we believe Him when Jesus says *'I will never leave you nor forsake you'* (Heb. 13:5)? If we can, His presence and glory should permeate our lives 24/7. And not only us. There could also be a foretaste of what He has promised, and that is to show the whole wide world his glory. A small and limited foreshadowing of this came in the Charismatic Movement of 1970s-1980s but that is now past.

We must ask: Are we are missing out on experiencing God's kingdom, power and glory today because we have overlooked what scripture says about it and failed to believe it? I believe that is indeed the case.

A personal story may explain. Sixteen years ago, at the Lord's behest I launched a website, *'Day of Christ Ministries'*, to share about this wonderful day He had showed me from scripture. A day in which the Lord will shine forth his glory for all the world to see. Since then, millions have viewed the website, but seemingly very few took the message to heart.

I wondered why. Surely if God was quickening truth about the *'day of Christ'* to me He would also quicken it to others? Yet an internet search revealed only two other websites majoring on promoting this truth, Otis Q. Sellers (SeedAndBread.Org) and Plainer Words Online Bible Studies by Tom Ballinger. While their websites partly remain both men have since passed on, leaving me, as far as I know, the only living publisher of *'day of Christ'* truth online.

I had already written and published three books on other subjects and was fixing to 'retire' when the Lord insisted that I write again in this book what He has shown me. Accordingly, as this may well be my last assignment before 'permanent retirement', I ask those who open its pages to read this book giving an ear to *'what the Spirit saith to the churches'* (Rev. 2:7).

I believe the message is timely and true but it does, and will, face opposition. You see, you might think news that God is going to bring in an age of great blessing to all on earth before the day of judgement (which is the *'day of the Lord'*) would be welcomed with open arms. That has not been the case.

I found it fell largely on deaf ears and both Otis Sellers and Tom Ballinger were publicly opposed and abused. Yet their essential message was based on what God said from the beginning and reiterated through his prophets. It was the core of Jesus's teaching at his first advent and was key to the gospel later preached by the apostles.

How that can be deemed heresy is incomprehensible to me. Why it is so rejected is easier to understand. It is because the devil, like the world, prefers bad news to good; in fact, he so hated the good news, the gospel Jesus proclaimed, he had Him crucified.

When every knee will bow

But back to the goodness of the *'day of Christ'* that we should be anticipating. Lasting several centuries this superb time of restoration and recreation will see most everybody on earth turned back to God, the curse of sin lifted, sickness banished and the earth returned to its pre-Flood beauty. (Again, the detail will be spelled out later).

Fact is, six times in most Bibles (seven in the KJV) the *'day of Christ'* is cited as the time of great blessing all believers should look forward to. (Please check out 1 Cor. 1:8, 1 Cor. 5:5 and 2 Cor. 1:14, Phil. 1:6, 1:10 and 2:16 and 2 Thess. 2:2, the latter only in the KJV).

In short, the *'day of Christ'* is a cosmic event of world recreating importance. It is when *'every knee shall bow and every tongue confess that Jesus Christ is Lord to the glory of God the Father'* (Phil. 2:10). It is when the Lord will rule from heaven and fill earth with his glory. It is when Jesus Christ the man is revealed in his full glory as *'the great God and our Saviour Jesus Christ'* (Titus 2:13) that He is.

And, no, this glorious event does not await either the so-called 'Rapture' or the 'Great Tribulation'. It does not require the *'man of sin, the antichrist'* to be manifest first, nor does it occur at the Lord's personal and physical return to earth, his *parousia* or so-called 'Second Coming'. Thankfully, the *'day of Christ'* comes before all that.

You see, it's not the 'rapture', nor the *'great and terrible day of the Lord'* (Joel 2:11) we should be looking for as God's next move. It's the Lord's **appearing** (Greek: *epiphaneia,* not *parousia).*

Matter of fact the word 'Rapture' is not found in scripture but the far more important word *'appearing'* frequently occurs. Jesus Himself spoke of his **appearing** (Matt. 24:30), and the Apostles Peter, John and Paul spoke of it as the essential hope for all believers.

Thus, in 1.Pet. 5:4 Peter speaks of the 'under-shepherds' who will receive glory when the *'chief Shepherd shall **appear***'. In 1 Peter. 1:7 he says the believer's *'trial of faith … might be found unto praise and honour and glory at the **appearing** of Jesus Christ'.*

The Apostle John urges his readers to *'Abide in Him that when He shall **appear** we may have confidence…'* (1 John 2:28). In 1 John

3:2 he writes '...*we know that when He shall **appear**, we shall be like Him, for we shall see Him as He is.*'

And, of course, Paul, the Apostle to the Gentiles, repeatedly points believers to the **appearing**. Indeed, in Titus 2:13 he urges that we should be '...*looking for that blessed hope and the glorious **appearing** of our great God and Saviour Jesus Christ.*'

So, let's pause to study just what the **appearing** is. In the passage Titus 2:11-13 the Apostle Paul makes plain just where we now are in God's timetable and what He will do next:

> *For the grace of God which brings salvation has **appeared** to all men, teaching us that, denying ungodliness and worldly lusts, we should **live** soberly, righteously and godly in this present age, **looking** for the **blessed hope** and **glorious Appearing** of our **great God and Saviour Jesus Christ**...*

We are living between these two '**appearings**' of the Lord, thanking God for the salvation of the first and urgently looking for the next. But, ask most church goers if they are looking for His **appearing** (Greek: *epiphaneia*, meaning a blazing forth of the Lord's glory) and they will say they're looking for the 'Rapture' and/or his 'Second Coming' instead. Yet neither are mentioned in the above passage, nor is the '*day of the Lord*'. Nor are they cited anywhere in the 'pastoral' epistles to Timothy and Titus.

What is clearly taught here, however, is our present place in God's purpose for the ages. As said, we are between the two **appearings** of Christ. In the **first** (vs. 11), He has **appeared** to us (and to all mankind) in the gospel of grace that brings salvation. In the **second** He is to **appear in** glory as the great God and Saviour Himself.

And such **appearing** is vital. Because, sadly, the God who became flesh to save us and has been exalted (as a man) to be God Almighty, the Saviour - '*For in Him dwells all the fullness of the Godhead* *dwelleth bodily'* (Col. 2:9) - is not recognised as such. Certainly not by the world but sadly also not by parts of the church. The doctrine that Christ is a man, having no pre-existence before his birth from Mary and therefore not the eternal God, is still held by many.

But it is as the great eternal God '*who was and is and is to come*' (Rev. 1:8) that the Lord Jesus Christ will manifest Himself at his second **appearing**. And that's not all. At this **appearing** He will both bring in his kingdom and judge the quick and the dead - that is He will inaugurate a centuries long programme of preserving the alive who turn to Him and raising the dead that are worthy (see 2 Tim. 4:1,8; 1 Peter 1:7).

Heralding this mighty event, the Apostle Paul urges us to be *'awaiting and looking for his **appearing**'* (Titus 2:13) which clearly, in his view, is the next thing to happen. But as already said, today most are looking instead for a 'Second Coming' (again a phrase that is foreign to scripture).

The upshot is that while there is no scripture mention of a 'Second Coming', the Bible clearly teaches that there is indeed a first and second '**appearing**' (Titus 2:11 and 13).

Now, many have speculated as to when the kingdom will come; that is, when the Lord will intervene to take over government of the world and rule over men. But 2 Tim. 4:1 mandates that it will come first at his **appearing**, not before and not afterwards in the *'day of the Lord'* (1 Thess. 5:2) when the Lord Jesus *'...shall be revealed from heaven with his mighty angels, in flaming fire taking vengeance on them that know not God and obey not the gospel of our Lord Jesus Christ'.*

Clearly the '*day of the Lord*' is a day of God's wrath and poured out judgement, and a later chapter will explain why. It is not a day when God abounds in blessing, restoration of all things, glory and widespread bestowing of eternal life. These two 'days' must be kept separate and not confused.

With the help of God, the blessing that comes from this understanding of both will be further explained in the chapters that follow.

Chapter Two - ARE WE STILL LOOKING FOR HIS APPEARING?

The answer to the above question for most of Christendom is apparently not. Although the Apostle Paul clearly teaches that the result of Christ **appearing** to us in saving grace (Titus 2:11) is that we should *'live soberly, righteously and godly, looking for that blessed hope and the glorious **appearing** in glory of the great God and our Saviour Jesus Christ'* (Titus 2:13), it seems most Christians aren't looking for it at all.

Rather they are convinced that Christ's appearing will occur only at what they call his 'Second Coming' (though no such actual phrase is found in scripture) and resolutely resist any suggestion that the **'appearing'** (Gk. e*piphanea*) is a separate and preceding event.

Yet there are several sound scriptural reasons to believe the Apostle Paul clearly saw the **appearing -** which literally means *'the blazing forth'* (of Christ's glory, that is) and is found in Titus 2:13, 2 Tim. 4:1, Col: 3:4, 1 Tim. 6:14, 2 Tim. 1:10, 4:1, 4:8 - as the time when he would receive from the Righteous Judge his reward, his inheritance.

Thus, *'in that day'* – the day of his *'appearing'* - the Lord would give Paul *'a crown of righteousness'* according to 2 Tim. 4:8 – and not to him only but also to *'all them also that love his appearing'*. Surely if he meant that he would receive this prize at the Lord's so-called 'Second Coming' or during the subsequent *'day of the Lord'* (1 Thess. 5:2), he would have said so. But he did not.

Secondly, there are two serious obstacles to holding that the Lord's personal physical return to earth is the next thing on God's agenda. The first is that before such a return of Christ (Gk. *parousia),* which means an official coming to take up residence in office and person and being greeted by a welcoming party (of resurrected saints who meet him in the air), see 1 Thess. 4:16, two other great events must occur:

1. There must be a great **falling away** first. (2 Thess. 2:3).
2. Then the man of lawlessness, the **son of perdition** must be revealed (also 2 Thess. 2: 3)

It can safely be said that neither of these terrible developments has occurred to date. Let us see why.

The first reason, simply put, is that before there can be a *'falling away'* there must be something good and perfect put in place by God to 'fall away' from. For example, when Adam and Eve sinned, they not only 'fell' from innocence into darkness and evil but their fall turned an earth created in perfection into a wilderness of weeds and thorns.

My point is that until 'the fall' the earth and all in it were perfect; indeed, God said that everything He had made was *'very good'* (Gen. 1:31). Man was also 'made very good', until he sinned. The point is clear: before there can be a 'fall' there must be something good and perfect to fall from.

So, when the future *'falling away'* takes place, it must also be from something that is *'very good'*. And, clearly, that cannot be the world which we live in now, for the Apostle Paul describes it as *'this present evil world'*. In fact, it is a world so wicked that Jesus died for our sins in order to *'deliver us'* from it. (Gal. 1:4)

You see, just as the *'tree of the knowledge of good and evil'* (Gen. 2:17) which Adam and Eve tasted could not produce good so the present *'evil'* age can only produce fruit that is evil in all who live in it. So much so, that even we who now believe in Christ our Saviour also once *'walked according to the course of this world'* and were led by *'the prince of the power of the air, the spirit that works in the children of disobedience'* (Eph. 2:2). We were by nature *'children of wrath'*, obstinate and rebellious and, if the truth be known, to some extent we still are.

Fact is that down the course of history whenever God has set up something good (such as the miracle-accompanied era of gospel proclamation in the Book of Acts, for example) man has 'fallen away' from it. Didn't Paul the Apostle of grace have to say that *'all they that be in Asia be turned away from me'* (2 Tim. 1:15) and didn't he weep because *'many walk ... as enemies of the cross of Christ'* (Phil. 3:18-19)?

What then is the 'good thing' God will establish before the *'falling away'* of 2 Thess. 2:3? It is my strong belief that this can only be that epoch which the Apostle Paul seven times describes as *'the day of Christ'* (see 1 Cor. 1:7, Phil. 2:16 and other references in his epistles).

This *'day of Christ'* is the pre-millennial, pre-advent age which was spoken of by all the Old Testament prophets, proclaimed as the *'kingdom of God'* or *'kingdom of Heaven'* then *'at hand'* by the Lord Jesus and later confirmed as a yet future event by the apostles Peter and Paul. It will be brought in by the '**appearing**' of Christ in a blaze of glory (Titus 2:13, 2 Tim. 4:1).

When God puts things right

The Apostle Peter called it *'the time of restitution of all things'* and said Christ would be retained in heaven until this stupendous global 'recreation' is accomplished (Acts 3:21). This *'day of Christ'* (also referred to by Paul as *'that day'* in his latter epistles) is, I submit, also the *'day of rest'* he referred to in Heb. 4:8-11).

What will it be like? Well, imagine a world of people freed from compulsion to sin, free from premature death, disease and war and living on an earth restored to its original created beauty and devoid of earthquakes, tempests, famine and pestilence. That is how it will be in this wonderful new day, which the Lord Jesus described as *'that world'* (Luke 20:35) and the Apostle Paul in Eph. 1:21 as *'the world to come'.*

In this *'day of Christ'* all government in the world will be taken over by God Himself in the person of the Lord Jesus Christ, the only *'Man'* deemed fit by God to rule in justice and equity over mankind (Ps. 98:9). He will rule from heaven over all people as the one and only king, a king of love, peace, righteousness and true justice. Importantly, the glory of Christ's kingdom – let's pause to remember the kingdom of heaven was the major theme of the Lord's teaching in his earthly ministry – will be brought about first at his **appearing**, not his final return to earth.

The glory of his **appearing** and his **kingdom** is summed up in these scriptures:

- 2 Tim. 4:1 proclaims that Christ will '*judge the quick and the dead at his **appearing** and his **kingdom**'.*
- 1 Tim. 6:14-16 speaks of '*... the **appearing** of our Lord Jesus Christ which in his times He shall show,* (He) *who is the blessed and only **Potentate*** (absolute ruler), *the King of kings and Lord of lords; Who only hath immortality dwelling in the light which no man can approach unto; Whom no man hath see, nor can see; to Whom be honour and power everlasting.'*
- Under the Lord's government '*in that day'*, tyranny, cruelty and exploitation, disease, poverty and death will be abolished, according to the Old Testament prophets. See the wonder of this set out in Ps. 67:

> *God be merciful to us and bless us, and cause his face to **shine** upon us. Selah. That thy **way** may be known upon earth, thy **saving health** among **all nations**. Let (cause) the people (to) praise Thee, O God; let all the people praise Thee. O let the nations be glad and sing for joy; for Thou shalt **judge** the people righteously, and **govern** the nations upon earth. Let the people praise Thee, O God; let (make) all the people praise Thee. Then shall the **earth** yield her **increase**; and God, even our own God, shall bless us. God shall bless us and all the ends of the earth shall fear Him.*

But just what is the '**falling away**'? The Greek word is *apostasia*, translated as *'falling away'* in the King James Bible, as *'rebellion'* in the NIV and RSV, and as *'apostasy'* in the Amplified Bible. It really means rebellion of the worst kind. And there cannot be such a severe rebellion unless:

A) First, the present dispensation of the grace of God (in which all men are potentially forgiven and reconciled to God if they trust Jesus as Saviour) has ended and a new arrangement in God's dealings with men takes its place, as the Apostle Paul said would be.

B) The long-promised government of God over earth, the *'day of Christ'* has been enacted and brought to bear from heaven upon earth as Jesus foretold in detail during his earthly ministry.

C) The powerful work of the Holy Spirit as the 'restrainer' *or 'withholder'* (2 Thess. 2:6), convincing *'the world of sin, righteousness and judgement'* (John 16:8) is withdrawn toward the end of the *'day of Christ'* as the Apostle Paul said would be.

The truth is that each age or *'world'* created by the Lord Jesus Christ (Heb. 1:2) has a consummation or ending. Thus, our Lord spoke of *'the end of the world'* - or age - (Matt. 24: 3, 14). The Apostle Paul spoke of *'the ends of the ages'* coming upon believers in the Acts period (1 Cor. 10:11). Sadly, the end, or consummation, of the *'day of Christ'* will come when the Holy Spirit the *'restrainer'* throughout this era of blessing is *'taken out of the way'* (2 Thess. 2:7).

Rebellion by some ensues and, though the saints are promised rest at this time, *'the lawless one will be revealed whom the Lord will consume with the breath of his mouth and destroy with the brightness of his coming* (2 Thess.1:7-8). Mark well, this occurs at his *parousia* at the start of the *'day of the Lord'* (1 Thess. 5:2), not at his *'appearing'* to usher in the *'day of Christ'* which by centuries precedes it.

Now to the second condition which has to be met before the terrible and destructive *'day of the Lord'* (Joel 2:11) is brought about by the return of the Lord in fiery judgement. This is the *'revealing'* of the *'man of sin'*, the *'lawless one'* who:

> *'…opposes and exalts himself above all that is called God or that is worshipped so that he sits in the temple of God, showing himself that he is God' (2 Thess. 2:4).*

Two points. Firstly, to be recognised as the *'man of sin'* he must be grossly wicked compared to others alive on earth at that time who do not rebel. (It would be hard to find such a stand out distinction in today's society since sin, even among them that name the name of Christ, is so widespread. But in the day of Christ, it will be very different – most everybody will know the Lord and obey Him – so a gross deceiver and rebel will stand out like a sore thumb to true believers.).

Secondly, it can be argued there must be a physical temple on earth and in Jerusalem for him to be *'revealed'* in (2 Thess. 2:8). And as yet no such temple has been built in Jerusalem, nor is it likely to be short of a huge change in the present disposition which sees Muslims occupying the temple site and the gate to the 'Holy of Holies' bricked up.

My conviction is that the religious conflict in the world which is centred in Jerusalem will not be changed until the Lord Jesus Christ reveals Himself as the rightful King of the earth at his *'appearing'* (Titus 2:13 and 2 Tim. 4:1). He will then rule over earth from heaven in what Paul calls the *'day of Christ'*. Later in his reign Israel will be restored to her rightful position and Elijah will *'come and restore all things'* (Matt. 17:11) including rebuilding the Jerusalem temple.

Given all that, then clearly the Lord's return to earth in physical, official presence, (*parousia*), his 'Second Coming' if you will, is still a far future, not imminent event. And without question the Lord's *'appearing'* (Gk. *epiphaneia*) is presented in scripture as an imminent event that precedes both Christ's physical return and the *'day of the Lord'*.

Thus, in Titus 2:13, the Apostle Paul specifically urges those saved by Christ's earlier *'appearing*' in saving grace for all people, not just Israel, (Titus 2:11) to be *'looking for his* (next) **appearing** *in glory as our great God and Saviour'*.

Had he meant the Lord's personal and physical return to earth in the *'day of the Lord'*, i.e., his 'second coming' surely, he would have said so.

Chapter Three -
IS THERE A CURE FOR OUR COMPLAINT?

Is there a cure for the malady of ineffectiveness that now afflicts the church? For, without question, today the Body of Christ is weak, unable to see many, if any, saved. No longer on fire for God, as it was 50 years ago in the Charismatic Movement, today it is deemed by many past its use-by date.

So, what's the cure? Revival, say those hungering for more of God, and they're right. But how we can we make revival come when only God can bring it about? What needs to happen for Him to again visit us and our world with a blaze of his Spirit in love and grace?

I suggest the answer may lie in turning to his Word to see if there's something we've missed out on - something that God wrote in his book long ago that his people have been blind to for centuries? You see, the Word of God has the answer to every situation. Whatever mess we or our world are in, scripture provides a remedy – if we will believe it. So, is there something we have forgotten that could bring relief to the church's and the world's present parlous condition?

Well, remember the two disciples, Cleopas and another, who walked sadly to Emmaus thinking that with Jesus dead there was no longer redemption for Israel (Luke 24: 13-31)? They couldn't believe He had risen from the dead as He said He would, even though angels had told women they knew He had done so. Why couldn't they believe? The reason, Jesus said, was that they were:

> *'...fools and slow of the heart to believe **all** that the prophets have spoken. Ought not Christ to have suffered these things and to enter into his glory?'* (Luke 24:25-26).

So, Cleopas and his fellow disciple were blind to Christ's glorious resurrection through not taking to heart *'**all** that the prophets have spoken'*. Importantly, they had forgotten the truth that after suffering and death their Messiah would *'enter into his glory'*. As 1 Pet. 1:11 teaches, the prophets of old searched…

> *'... what, or what manner of time, the **Spirit of Christ**, which was in them, did signify when it testified beforehand the sufferings of Christ and the glory to follow.'*

In our time, some 2,000 years later, it can safely be said the church at large has yet to *'believe all that the* (Old Testament) *prophets have spoken'*. Indeed, she has yet to acknowledge as true all that Jesus as a prophet Himself has said, let alone the many truths He later proclaimed through his apostles.

And the crux of the issue for us, just as it was for the two Emmaus disciples to whom Jesus revealed Himself, is what we believe about Christ's glory. The disciples couldn't believe in it until the Lord showed them a glimpse of his risen self in glory. And today, it seems, neither can the world nor even we.

Of course, we later believers know that Christ did indeed rise from the dead and sat down at the right hand of the Father in glory. We also understand that now *'...our life is hid with Christ in God'* (Col. 3:3). But have we gone on to believe that, *'When Christ who is our life shall appear, we shall appear with Him in glory'* (Col. 3:4)?

Do we believe *'all that the prophets have spoken'*, all that the whole Bible has to say about the glorious day when Christ Jesus will shine forth his glory in his own right as God Almighty? This day is the *'day of Christ'*, (again 1 Cor. 1:8, 5:5, Phil. 1:10, 2:16, etc.) the great day of blessing for mankind that is ignored as a separate event by nearly all modern end time schemes of biblical interpretation.

'In that day' Christ will be seen for who He truly is, the only image of the '*one true God'* (John 17:3), the *'ancient of days'*, Creator of all things, the Lord of heaven and earth and Redeemer of all who trust Him to save them. He is God Almighty, *'For in Him dwelleth all of the fullness of the Godhead bodily'* (Col. 2:9).

The *'day of Christ'* is the day when He will sit on his own throne, *'the throne of his glory'* (Matt. 25:31), not sit just at the right hand of the Father's throne (compare Heb. 8:1, 12:2 with Matt. 19:28 and Acts 2:30). It is the day of his **appearing** in the fullness of being God in his own right (Titus 2:13). Sadly, the prevailing view among Christians is that the *'day of Christ'* and His *'appearing'* (Titus 2:13) is not a separate and preceding day to the *'day of the Lord'* (1 Thess. 5:2) as scripture clearly implies, but merely a part of what is called his 'Second Coming' and thus part of the *'day of the Lord'*.

Consequently, it can be truly said that today most of Christendom is failing to believe all that the prophets have said. The popular end time view has set aside clear scripture in both the Old and New Testaments that teach there will be a great day of blessing in which the Lord will shine forth his glory to melt hearts, remove mountains and bring in his kingdom to take over rule of the world. All this, including the sending again of the Prophet Elijah, will occur **'before** *that great and terrible day of the Lord'* (Joel 2:11 and Mal. 4:5).

A simple Bible study of the phrase *'in that day'* will show that there are two great days – one of great blessing, glory and mercy', the other of death, destruction and the vengeance of God. Here's a sampling:

Scriptures describing the day of blessing

Isa. 29:18-19 - *And **in that day** shall the deaf hear the words of the book and, and the eyes of the blind shall see out of obscurity, and out of darkness. The meek shall increase their joy in the Lord and the poor among men shall rejoice in the Holy One of Israel.*

Hos. 2:18 - *And **in that day** I will make a covenant for them with the beasts of the field and with the fowls of heaven and with the creeping things of the ground and I will break the bow and the sword and the battle out of the earth and will make them to lie down safely.*

Joel 3:18 - *And it shall come to pass **in that day** that the mountains shall drop down new wine, and the hills shall flow with milk, and all the rivers of Judah shall flow with waters, and a fountain shall come forth of the house of the Lord and shall water the valley of Shittim.*

Isa. 24:21 - *And it shall come to pass **in that day** the Lord shall punish the host of the high ones that are on high and the kings of the earth upon the earth.*

Zech. 2:11 - *And many nations shall be joined unto the Lord **in that day**, and shall be my people: and I will dwell in the midst of thee and thou shalt know that the Lord of Hosts has sent Me.*

Zech. 9:16-17 - *And the Lord God shall save them **in that day** as the flock of his people: for they shall be as the stones of a crown, lifted up as an ensign upon his land. For how great is his goodness, and how great is his beauty! Corn shall make the young men cheerful, and new wine the maids.*

Scriptures describing the day of vengeance

> Zeph. 1:15-17 - *That day is a day of wrath, a day of trouble and distress, a day of wasteness and desolation, a day of darkness and gloominess, a day of clouds and thick darkness. … And I will bring distress upon men that they shall walk as blind men, because they have sinned against the Lord and their blood shall be poured out as dust, and their flesh as the dung.*

> Amos 8:3 - *And the songs of the temple shall be howlings **in that day**, saith the Lord God: there shall be many dead bodies in every place: they shall cast them forth with silence.*

> Ezek. 38:19 - *For in my jealousy and in the fire of my wrath have I spoke. Surely, **in that day** there shall be a great shaking in the land of Israel.*

> Isa. 2:10-11 - *Enter into the rock and hide thee in the dust, for fear of the Lord and the glory of his majesty. The lofty looks of man and the haughtiness of men shall be bowed down, and the Lord alone shall be exalted **in that day**.*

Can you see the difference? Which day would you want to see God bring upon the troubled world, the day of blessing or the day of his wrath? Both are true; both will occur but one comes before the other. My conviction is that in his next move God will bring his day of blessing, the *'day of Christ'* before anything else. Only after centuries of this wonderful era, when towards the end the Holy Ghost eases his restraint and is *'taken out of the way'* and rebellion by mankind breaks out again, will the Lord return *'…in flaming fire taking vengeance on them that know not God and, and that obey not the gospel of our Lord Jesus Christ'* (2 Thess. 1:7-8).

Our God is a God of goodness, mercy and grace. What good would it do for Him to visit death and destruction upon our already deeply troubled world after showing it such wonderful grace and long-suffering for so long in order to save individuals in the present era? Rather, I suggest He will stay true to his character and, in order to save the world as the Bible says, He will first pour out his richest blessing yet on the human race?

Against my view, it is commonly held, that there is only one great future day, the *'day of the Lord'* (1 Thess. 5:2) and that the *'day of Christ'* should be fitted into it. However, as the next chapter will show, the *'day of Christ'* cannot be made to fit within the *'day of the Lord'*. Its promises are too wonderful for that.

Chapter Four - ENLIGHTENMENT IN THE DAY OF CHRIST

> Ps. 97: 4 - *His lightnings enlightened the world, the earth saw and trembled.*
>
> Isa. 29:18 - *And in that day (i.e., the day of Christ) shall the deaf hear the words of the book and the eyes of the blind shall be see out of obscurity and out of darkness.*

We may not see our world this way but in God's view it is a dark, evil place. He sees it as a world of '*night*' (John 9:4) in which '*no man can work*'. Indeed, so dark is its sin that enlightened, grace-saved believers are strictly warned by the Apostle Paul to '*have no fellowship (at all) with the unfruitful works of darkness*' (Eph. 5:11).

So much for the bad news. The good news is that God deeply loves the world; so much so He sent his only begotten Son to save it. And because He loves it so much very soon God will send dazzling **enlightenment** to the whole world. In that day people will no longer have '*eyes that can't see and ears that can't hear*'. For in the '*day of Christ*' all will see the Lord Jesus Christ manifest in glory and all will hear his voice.

This **enlightenment** will be brought to the world by his '*appearing*'. But before we again turn the spotlight on that, let's affirm afresh that we, as grace-saved believers, have already been made individually to 'see the light'. Eph. 1:18 says that we who have believed the Apostle Paul's report are '*enlightened that ye may know what is the hope of his calling and what the riches of the glory of his inheritance in the saints*'.

What's more, those quickened to learn the *'mystery'* truth of Paul's prison epistles know that they have been *'made meet to be partakers of the inheritance of the saints in light* (and) ... *delivered from the power of darkness'* (Eph. 1:12-13). Right now then we should be rejoicing in grace and learning to *'walk as (the) children of light'* that God has made us to be (Eph. 5:8).

But for the vast majority of mankind, it's a desperately darker story. Thank God we live in New Zealand, where courtesy of gospel preaching for over a century we enjoy peace, safety, freedom to worship and reasonable provision. Contrast that with the lot of folk in pagan, idol worshipping countries:

Ten per cent of Indian people are deemed slaves and on Ross Kemp's 'Extreme World' television programme an Indian procurer casually admitted killing, as a matter of course, hundreds of young girls kidnapped for prostitution once they had passed their 'use by date'. In the Catholic Philippines a third of people live in hunger. And in the Mediterranean thousands of refugees fleeing war and poverty on leaky ships are abandoned to drowning by Indonesia, Malaysia and Thailand. And now Russia has invaded the Ukraine to end that nation's freedom to pursue its own destiny.

A dark world indeed. That's why for the sake of all humanity, as well as for ourselves, we should be eagerly looking for his **'appearing'** (Titus 2:13). Indeed, it is for the very purpose of looking for '*his appearing'* that God saved us by grace in the first place (Titus 2:12).

So, what is the **appearing?** The word translates *epiphaneia* which means to powerfully shine forth. **Enlightenmen**t in the Bible then is not the flowering of artistic creativity nor a more rational approach as in the humanly supposed 'Age of Enlightenment'. Rather it is the shining forth of the glory of a person, the Lord Jesus Christ. More piercing than a searchlight, brighter than the noon-day sun (Acts 22:6, 26:13) his *'appearing'* will truly light up the world.

Consider these scriptures:

> Psa. 77:18 - *The voice of thy thunder was in the heaven: the **lightnings lightened** the world: the earth trembled and shook.*

> Isa. 40:5 - *And the glory of the Lord shall be **revealed** and all flesh shall **see** it together for the mouth of the Lord hath spoken it.*

> Isa. 49:26 - *...and all flesh shall know that **know** that I am the Lord.*

> Joel 2:28, Acts 2:17 - *I will **pour out** my Spirit on all flesh.*

> Ps. 98:2 - *All flesh shall **see** the salvation of God.*

> Isa. 52:10 - *All the ends of the earth shall **see** the salvation of our God.*

> Isa. 29:18 - *And in that day (i.e., the 'day of Christ') shall the deaf **hear** the words of the book and the **eyes** of the blind shall **see** out of obscurity and out of darkness. The meek also shall increase their joy in the Lord and the poor among men shall rejoice in the Holy One of Israel.*

All this will happen in the '*day of Christ*' (Phil. 1:6, 1:10 and 2:16). Right now, however, '*Christ is hid with God*' and we with Him (Col. 3:3) but when He **appears** it will be in a blaze of such glory that all will know Him and have their hearts changed by Him.

You see, while Jesus was the '***light*** *of the world*' when He walked among men in Israel, that was the light of the Son of Man, the earthly Messiah. But men preferred darkness to light as they still do today. Christ then did not then **appear** in his full glory at that time. Rather, Phil. 2:7 says that '*He made Himself of no reputation and took upon Him the form of a servant and was made in the likeness of men*'.

Now, on the Damascus road, Paul was blinded by but the briefest glimpse of the **glory** of the ascended, glorified Lord (Acts 9:1-9, 22:6-10, 26:12-19) but neither he nor anyone else has yet seen the Mediator '*the man Christ Jesus*' **appear** in his full glory as '*the great God and our Saviour*' (Titus 2:13) that God has made Him. This because right now '*Christ is hid with God*' (Col. 3:3). But we will so see Him if we are '*looking for*' and '*love*' his **appearing** (2 Tim. 4:8).

What is it like to see the Lord in his full **glory** as King of heaven and earth? John and Daniel fell at his feet as though dead when they but glimpsed his **glory** as the earth's true King. However, it seems Isaiah was carried forward to look far into the future to see the Lord as He will be revealed in glory and ruling on high in the '*day of Christ*' (Isa. 6:1-5):

> *In the year that king Uzziah died I* **saw** *also the Lord sitting upon a throne, high and lifted up, and his train filled the temple. Above it stood the seraphim: each one had six wings; with twain he covered his face and with twain he covered his feet and with twain he did fly. And one cried unto another and said, Holy, holy, holy is the Lord of hosts; the whole earth is full of his* **glory**.

Notice below the prophet's reaction to what he saw.

> *Then said I, Woe is me, for I am undone: because I am a man of unclean lips, and I dwell in the midst of a people of unclean lips: for mine eyes have seen the King!*

Then realise that in the '*day of Christ*' the world's billions will feel exactly as Isaiah did when they too **see** the King. They will abhor themselves when they **see** the light of his holiness. Yes, people everywhere will immediately realise their sin and need of salvation when Christ shines Himself forth in the full glory of God. Isaiah, holy prophet though he was, crumpled in the face of it.

The Apostle Paul wrote of this hugely humbling and **enlightening** experience in Phil. 2:10-11:

> *That at the name of Jesus every knee should bow of things in heaven and things in earth and things under the earth. And that every tongue should confess that Jesus Christ is Lord to the glory of God the Father.*

My late friend Bible teacher Tom Ballinger wrote that in the *'day of Christ'*, at his **appearing**, 'everyone one will be **enlightened** concerning all spiritual matters including knowing exactly who Jesus Christ is … that is, God Almighty'. In that day, "How could I have gotten it so wrong, how could I have been so blind, so deceived?" will be the cry of many.

The *'day of Christ'* is a theme that flows through the Bible. It is the time when the Lord Jesus Christ is revealed both in heaven and in earth as the God who made Himself man that as man, He might be made God to save us. It is when Christ will show Himself forth as the true and only king of heaven and earth. Which is why in 1 Tim. 6: 14-15 Paul urges Timothy:

> *That thou keep this commandment without spot, unrebukeable, until the **Appearing** of our Lord Jesus Christ, which in his times He shall shew, Who is the blessed and only Potentate the King of kings and Lord of lords.*

At his **appearing** our Lord will show everyone who is the world's real and only ruler – that is, Himself. Satan at this time will no longer continue as '*the god of this world*'. Notice our Lord's **appearing** takes place '*in his times*', i.e., in his day, the '*day of Christ*'; '*my day*' as He called it in John 8:56. And, as said, the New Testament mentions the '*day of Christ*' by name in seven places. They are: 2 Thess. 2:2, 1 Cor. 1:8, 1 Cor. 5:5, 2 Cor. 1:14, Phil. 1:6, 1:10 and 2:16.

Importantly, in his shining forth as King, Christ will not only show the devil what's what, but all the angels in heaven and people on earth as well. None will be able to stand against the **light** of his **glory**.

Study for yourself these further scriptures on the **appearing**: 1 Tim. 6:14-15, Col. 3:3-4, 2 Tim. 4:1, Titus 2:11-13. In 2 Tim. 4:1 Christ's **appearing** is clearly linked to the manifestation of his '*heavenly kingdom*':

> *I charge thee therefore before God and the Lord Jesus Christ who shall judge the quick and the dead at his **appearing** and his **kingdom**. And the Lord shall deliver me from every evil work and preserve me unto his **heavenly kingdom**.*

Five times in scripture (including Isa. 6:3) it is recorded that the whole earth will be filled with his **glory**. Five is the number of grace and thus it is in grace that Christ will rule from heaven. It helps our understanding to know that the prayers of the prophets are prophetic in that they foretell future events that will certainly happen. These 'glory' verses are listed below.

> Isa. 6:3 - *And one cried unto another, and said, Holy, holy, holy is the Lord of Hosts, The whole earth is full of his glory.*

> Num. 14:21 - *But as truly as I live all the earth shall be filled with the **glory of the Lord**.*

> Ps. 72:18-19 - *(the prophetic prayer of David): Blessed be the Lord God, the God of Israel who only doeth wondrous things and blessed be his glorious name for ever and let the whole earth be filled with his **glory**.*

> Isa. 11:9 - *They shall not hurt nor destroy in all my holy mountain, for the whole earth shall be full of the **knowledge** of the Lord as the waters cover the sea.*

Hab. 2:14 - *For the earth shall be filled with the* **knowledge** *of the glory of Lord as the waters cover the sea.*

Chapter Five -
THE DAY OF MAN AND THE DAY OF CHRIST

We live in the **day of man**. Man sits in judgment and his opinions are held sacrosanct. Never mind that his views defy both logic and the Bible, they must be believed. Education, science, false religion, the law and Government all demand that God-denying theories and false beliefs be taught and accepted.

Actually, for some six thousand years now man has sat in judgment on the truth of God and in his view found it wanting. From Eve's heeding the serpent whispering "*yea, hath God said?*" in Gen. 3:1 through to the late physicist Stephen Hawking's pronouncement that modern science makes God 'redundant in the creation of the universe', man has always made up his own story, or followed that of the devil, as he goes along.

Nimrod led all mankind in rebellion after the Flood and built the tower of Babel. As folklore around the world records, he 'pushed back the sky' to make room for man to dwell beneath it without heeding the commandments or truth of God.

But it was when the rulers of Israel came to arrest, try and crucify Jesus, the Son of Man, that the **day of man** reached its zenith of wickedness. The Lord told them:

> *Be ye come out, as against a thief, with swords and staves? When I was daily with you in the temple ye stretched forth no hands against Me: but this is your* **hour** *(hora, Strong's 5610, primarily meaning* **day)** *and the power of darkness (Luke 22:53).*

Jesus was saying that because this was the **day of man** the satanically inspired Jewish religious leaders were able to take and crucify Him. It was 'their day' then and it is still their day, **man's day**, now. But, watch out, his day, the **day of Christ**, is coming.

As we have seen, the *'day of Christ'* is mentioned in several places in Paul's epistles. What's more, all the Old Testament prophets spoke of this glorious day when Christ will reign from heaven, men's hearts will be turned toward Him and the earth and all creatures in it will be restored to their original creation beauty.

Sadly, right now we still live in the **day of man**. Today, as he has for thousands of years man judges God, his servants and the truth of his Word the Bible, and finds fault with them. Now, as then, he dismisses as idiots those who believe God's word and persecutes them. But very soon it will be God's turn to judge because a great **new day** is coming. The *'day of judgement'*, also called the *'day of Christ'* will give mankind a divine 'check up from the neck up'.

Now, let me ask, what do the words *'day of judgement'* bring to mind? Do you envisage people suddenly being sent either to heaven or hell? Or does an image of people being killed and the earth being burnt up cross your mind? Can I suggest you join me in a Bible study which will show another picture? For the *'day of judgment*, the *'day of Christ'*, is really about changing man's thinking rather than sending him to hell. For the good news is that this new era of God dispensing Himself into mankind will be more about putting things right rather than damning those who have got it wrong.

Prov. 23:7 says of man that *'as he thinketh in his heart, so is he'*. And Shakespeare echoes this thought, writing that 'there is nothing good or bad but thinking makes it so'. All the corruption, violence, poverty and evil in the world can be traced back to one root cause: 'stinking thinking' that determinedly leaves God out of the equation. As the Psalmist has it, *'The fool hath said in his heart there is no God'*.

So, what does the Bible say about this coming **day of judgement**? What does it say about the '**day of man**' and his judgement in the '**day of Christ**'? Turn to 1 Cor. 4:4-5 where the Apostle Paul writes:

> *But with me it is a very small thing that I should be judged of you, or of **man's judgement**: yea I judge not my own self. For I know nothing by myself; yet am I not hereby justified: but He that judgeth me is the Lord.*
>
> *Therefore judge nothing **before the time**, until **the Lord come**, who both will bring to light the hidden things of darkness, and will make manifest the counsels of the heart: and then shall every man have praise of God.*

An important difference

It's important to realise that 1 Cor. 4:5 is not describing the Lord's 'Second Coming'. Those who think it does make the mistake of confusing the Lord's **appearing** in the **day of Christ** with his **coming** during the tribulation to bring in the **day of the Lord**. **Appearing** is *epiphanea*, Strong's 2015, meaning a manifestation or shining forth. It describes the time when Christ will shine forth from heaven (Titus 2:13. 2 Tim. 4:1). In contrast, **coming** (as in his second coming), is *parousia*, Strong's 3952, meaning a full personal and official **coming** and **staying**. It denotes the Lord's physical coming to earth to '*rule with a rod of iron*' in his millennial reign.

However, in 1 Cor. 4:5 the word '**come**' - as in *'until the Lord come'* - is neither *epiphanea* nor *parousia*. It is *erchomai*, Strong's 2064, which basically means to 'come and go' but can also mean '*appear*' for it is at his appearing that He will inaugurate his heavenly rule over earth (2 Tim. 4:1). And the use of it in 1 Cor. 4:4-5 makes clear that is in the **day of Christ** that the judgement Paul speaks of takes place.

For, while ruling and reigning from heaven in his *'heavenly kingdom'* (2 Tim. 4:1), Christ will also 'come and go' to visit the earth at times. Proof of that is found in Ezekiel where the door to the east is reserved for the '*Prince*' (of glory), i.e. Christ, to come in (Ezek. 43: 1-4) and in Malachi:

> *The Lord whom ye seek shall suddenly come to his temple, even the messenger of the covenant in whom ye delight... (Mal. 3:1).*

This latter prophecy was not exhausted by the Lord's first coming and his cleansing of the temple. It will be further fulfilled in the **day of Christ** when the Lord visits his resurrected apostles and Old Testament saints in a rebuilt temple in Jerusalem to have communion with them.

Remember He said he would no more eat of the Passover or drink of the fruit of the vine *'until the kingdom of God shall come'* (Luke 22:16-18). Importantly, the kingdom of God comes into being in the **day of Christ** at the Lord's **appearing.** Read this in Titus 2:13 and 2 Tim. 4:1 which says:

> *I charge thee therefore before God and the Lord Jesus Christ who shall* **judge** *the quick and the dead at his* **appearing** *and his* **kingdom.**

By the way, may I ask, do you have a King James Bible? If so, I hope you have a 'good' and not 'naughty' one. What I mean by that is that a 'good' KJB version has the original margin notes of the 1611 translation while a 'naughty' one does not. So, it's 'naughty' because it does not tell 'the whole truth'. The distinction is clearly seen in the words '*man's judgement*' in 1 Cor.4:4. In the 'good' KJB the margin note reads 'Lit. **day**', but in the 'naughty' version it is omitted. Put the margin note *'day'* together with '*man's judgement*' in the text and you have *'man's day of judgement'* which fits and fully bears out the context of 1 Cor. 4:1-7.

The thrust of Paul's teaching here is that rather than negatively judging Paul and his fellow workers the Corinthians should consider them as *'ministers of Christ and stewards of the mysteries of God'*. The apostle is Christ's servant and merely obeys the Master's orders. He is also a steward (dispenser) of the mysteries (hitherto hidden secrets now revealed) and should be respected as such. Unwarranted criticism, based on ignorance, ceases when God's apostles are viewed in this light.

Ultimately, true judgement of a servant can be determined only by the Lord and that will only happen in *'the day'* (i.e., the *'day of Christ'*) when He brings to light the hidden things of darkness and makes manifest the counsels of the hearts. In other words, God's judgement of ministers (indeed of all men) is postponed until the **appearing** of the Lord Jesus Christ *'who shall judge the quick and the dead at his **appearing** and kingdom'* (2 Tim. 4:1). And this, of course, takes place in the *'day of Christ'*.

When man will be in the dock

This is why Paul says that to him it is a very small thing that he should be judged as an apostle (or criticised) by the Corinthians, or critically dismissed by the world in this, the day of *'man's judgement'* (vs. 3). He further explains that he does not even judge (that is, critically assess) himself. *'For I know nothing of* (or against*) myself yet I am not hereby justified but He that judgeth me is the Lord'*. If even Paul as an apostle is not judged by the Lord in this, the *'day of man's judgement'*, then neither should man judge him *'before the time'*, he argues.

Discerning Bible students will see a golden nugget of truth in 1 Cor. 4:3-5. It is that while for some 6,000 years it has been *'man's day of judgment'*, the *'day of Christ'* (Phil. 1:6, 10 and 2:16), which is the start of 'God's day of judgement', is now at hand. In this day there will be true judgement for, unlike man, the Lord judges after the heart and not the outward appearance. He weighs the motives not the mistakes, the believer's faith not his failures. For example, the Lord considered David a man after his own heart and one who by faith in God served his generation. Yet David was also a self-confessed murderer and adulterer.

In this **day of judgement,** it will not be God but man that is in the dock. Man at large will be charged and found guilty. Humanity's lofty thoughts and proud institutions will be brought crashing down; the political and economic systems will implode; hierarchies will topple, and worship of God '*in spirit and in truth*' (John. 4:23) will replace present man-made religious systems. And God will do all this in true fairness and love. Even the rebellious will be blessed. Ps. 68:18 - ...*Thou hast received gifts for men, yea for the rebellious also, that the Lord God might dwell among them*'.

It is this '*day of judgement*', i.e., the '*day of Christ*', that the Apostle Paul told the Athenian philosophers about in Acts 17:30-31:

> ...*God is now declaring to men that all everywhere should repent, because He has fixed* **a day** *in which He will judge the world in righteousness through a man He has appointed, having furnished proof by raising Him from the dead (NASB).*

The day God has fixed is, of course, the '*day of Christ*' and his call is that men should now repent in light of its imminent arrival. You see, God is not yet judging the world. If He were the Holy Spirit would indeed be convicting '...*the world of sin, righteousness and judgement*' (John 16:8). A mere glance at the day's news clearly shows that right now He is not, since often wickedness and evil seem to flourish unchecked. But He will – in the '*day of Christ*', the day of judgement.

Now, it is a principle with God that *'judgement must begin at the house of God'* (1 Pet. 4:17) and that will also be true in the *'day of Christ'*. A picture of how God will judge Christendom for its rejection of His grace and truth is amply set out in the epistles of the Apostle Paul. In 1 Cor. 3:13, for example, Paul teaches that:

> *Every man's work shall be made manifest: for the* **day** *(that is, the* **day of Christ***) shall declare it, because it shall be revealed by fire, and the fire shall try every man's work of what sort it is.*

'The day' mentioned here must be the *'day of Christ'*, since it is mentioned as such in the context (see 1 Cor. 1:8). And in the *'day of Christ'* religious Christendom with all its pomp and ceremony, lies and corruption will be burned up. Responsible for keeping millions from true faith in Christ some denominations will vanish in a puff of smoke. But those who have truly believed, though their works be burned up, will be preserved through the fire.

The upshot is that only that which has been truly founded on Christ, found in Christ and built by God Himself will survive when tried by the fire in the *'day of Christ'*.

Now, *'…a day is with the Lord as a thousand years'* (2 Pet. 3:8). This is not speaking of a 24-hour day but of an eon, an epoch lasting several centuries. For the record there are four great days that are mentioned in scripture, some lasting longer than others. They are:

- The day of man - 1 Cor. 3:13, 1 Cor. 4:3, Luke 22:53.
- The day of Christ - Rom. 2:5, 13:12-13, 1 Cor. 1:8, 1 Cor. 3:13, Phil. 1:10, 2:16, 2 Thess. 2:2, Eph. 4:30, Tim. 1:12, 18, 4:8, Heb. 4:7-8, 10:25
- The day of the Lord – 1 Thess. 5:2, Joel 2:1, 2 Pet. 3:10.
- The day of God - 2 Pet. 3:12, Rev. 16:14.

Chapter Six -
TWO INTO ONE WON'T GO

As already said, the prevailing end time view in in Christianity is that the *'day of Christ'* and the *'day of the Lord'* are one and the same, virtual synonyms for the same event. But the scriptural truth is that 'two into one won't go'. Neither will three – and there are three great days in God's timetable – the day of Christ (1 Cor. 1:8), the day of the Lord (1 Thess. 5:2) and the day of God (2 Pet. 3:12 and Rev. 16:14).

You see, unless the first two of these great days in God's unfolding programme of the ages are treated as separate and successive events, then no place can be found for some of his greatest promises to be fulfilled.

If you doubt that just try fitting the wonderful blessings for the world God speaks of in the scriptures below into the '*day of the Lord*' passages in 1 and 2 Thess., 1 and 2 Pet. and in Revelation. It immediately becomes clear that universal blessing and vengeful destruction worldwide simply don't mix:

> Ps. 67:4 - *O let the nations be glad and sing for joy for Thou shalt judge the people righteously and govern the nations upon earth.*
>
> Isa. 29:18 - *And in that day shall the deaf hear the words of the book and the eyes of the blind shall see out of obscurity and out of darkness. The meek also shall increase their joy in the Lord and the poor among men shall rejoice in the Holy One of Israel.*
>
> Ps. 98:2 - *All flesh shall see the salvation of God.*

> Isa. 11:9 - *They shall not hurt nor destroy in all my holy mountain, for the whole earth shall be full of the knowledge of the Lord as the waters cover the sea.*

Where can a place be found for these blessed promises to all mankind in scriptures such as the following?

> 1 Thess. 5:2-3 - *For you, yourselves, know perfectly well that the day of the Lord so comes as a thief in the night. For when they say 'Peace and safety!' then sudden destruction comes upon them…*
>
> 2 Thess. 1:7-8 - *…when the Lord Jesus is revealed from heaven with his mighty angels, in flaming fire taking vengeance on those who know not God and on those who do not obey the gospel of our Lord Jesus Christ, who shall be punished with everlasting destruction from the presence of the Lord and from the glory of his power.*
>
> 2 Pet. 3:7 - *But the heaven and the earth by his word are reserved for fire, kept for the day of judgement and destruction of ungodly men.*
>
> 2 Pet. 3:10 - *But the day of the Lord will come like a thief, in which the heavens will pass away with a roar and the elements will be destroyed with intense heat, and the earth its works will be burned up.*

Now, in 1 Thess. 5:1 the Apostle Paul said he had no need to write to the Thessalonians concerning the '*times and seasons, for you yourselves know perfectly well …*' But that is far from the case today among believers. They do not know the different timing of the '*day of Christ*' as opposed to the later '*day of the Lord*'.

Why? Because, influenced by pagan philosophies, the church has often set aside the plain teachings of scripture in favour of more worldly interpretations. Take, for example, the clear commandment of Jesus in Matt. 6:33: '*But seek ye **first** the kingdom of God and his righteousness and all these things shall be added unto to you*'.

Jesus meant his words to be taken literally. Before worrying about what to eat or wear his disciples should seek first to see God's kingdom brought upon earth. This instruction was reinforced by the Lord's instruction to **first** pray, '*thy kingdom come*' before asking, '*give us this day our daily bread*'. And the same priority – to seek **first** the kingdom of God – applies to understanding God's programme of future events.

Jesus did not say, seek **first** the '*day of the Lord*', but that is what most theologians do when it comes to end time interpretation. The Apostle Paul knew better. He tells us to seek **first** the kingdom of God that would come at Christ's **appearing** (Titus 2:13) to usher in the '*day of Christ*'. In Titus 2:13 we are told to be '*looking for the appearing of our great God and Saviour Jesus Christ*'. And 2 Tim. 4:1 makes clear this means the kingdom, saying:

> *...the Lord Jesus Christ ... will judge the quick and the dead at his Appearing and his kingdom*

Far from seeking **first** the kingdom, Christendom at large has for most of the last 2,000 years thought the church itself was the kingdom. Only the 'holy catholic church' could administer salvation to sinners, it was held, thus usurping the pre-eminence that rightly belongs only to the Lord Jesus Christ.

Thy kingdom come on earth

As to end time events the apostles' clear teaching that there would be a '*day of Christ*' followed by the '*day of the Lord*' was replaced by an unscriptural, one time 'last judgement' consigning all humanity either to heaven or hell and burning up the earth they once lived on.

In sharp contrast Jesus taught us to pray 'thy kingdom come … on earth'. For it is on earth that God will ultimately dwell with people (see Rev. 21:3 and Ps. 132:13-14). The widespread notion of people going to live for ever in heaven when they die is refuted by the clear Bible teaching saints will be resurrected back on earth. See Job 19:25-27 and John 6:40.

Of course, in two senses the kingdom is already with us. The very prospect of the Lord's certain rule over the world one day even now gives us this kingdom's 'righteousness, peace and joy in the Holy Ghost' (Rom. 14:17) in our hearts. And though the devil is running the 'present evil world' in which we live God has never vacated the throne of his sovereign rule over all. That said, please remember that Jesus taught that in the kingdom He, God, would rule the world and bring in a glorious world to come.

It is this world, brought in by the Lord's appearing at the dawn of the 'day of Christ', that the Apostle Paul foresaw when he told the Athenians that: *'He (God) has appointed a day in which He will judge the world in righteousness by the Man He has ordained…'* (Acts 17:31).

And very soon He will.

Chapter Seven -
THE DAY OF CHRIST AND OUR SALVATION

Fact is, six times in most Bibles the '*day of Christ*' is cited as the time of great blessing all believers should look forward to. Just when will we be fully and finally saved? This chapter seeks to address this important question in the light of what the Bible says in six verses about the Day of Christ. First though, perhaps we need to realise we are as yet in the process of being saved; it is not yet a completed work.

This the Apostle Paul made clear in Rom. 13:11, saying, '*Now is our salvation nearer than when we first believed*'. So, neither he nor his hearers were fully saved at that time but they were looking for a 'day' when they would be. Thus verses 11 and 12 read:

> *And knowing the **time**, that it is now **high time** to wake out of sleep for now is our salvation nearer than when we first believed. The night is far spent, the **day** is at hand: let us therefore cast off the works of darkness, and let us put on the armour of light.*

Notice, nearly 2,000 years ago believers were 'asleep' to the truth that day of Christ was '*at hand*' because they did not know the timing. They were asleep then and we as the church, Christ's body, seem asleep to it now. But we need to wake up, believe all that the Lord and his prophets and apostles have said and love our neighbour, cast off the works of darkness and put on the truth of the '*the day of Christ*' as our '*armour of light*'. Above all, we need to be '*looking for his appearing*' (Titus 2:13) because this will begin '*the day*' of our full salvation.

Already, we are sealed with the *'Holy Spirit of promise'*, God's down-payment against that *'day'* when we will be fully purchased, fully redeemed, *'body, soul and spirit'* (1 Thess. 5:23) and resurrected to live again on earth in Christ's kingdom. And that day, I submit, is the *'day of Christ'*. This truth teaches that today we only have a small deposit of the Spirit. How glorious it will be to live in the fullness of the Spirit in the day to come.

Blameless in the day of his revelation

But back to how scripture presents the *'day of Christ'* as the time when this will happen. The first mention of the term is in **1 Cor. 1:7-8** which in the NIV reads:

> *Therefore you do not lack any spiritual gift as you eagerly wait for our Lord Jesus Christ to be revealed. He will keep you strong to the end so that you will be blameless on* **the day of our Lord Jesus Christ.**

Note that in verse 7 the *'coming'* of the King James Version is here more correctly translated as *'revelation'*. Indeed, nearly all bibles translate the Greek word *apokulapsis* as 'revealing' or 'manifestation' (Douay-Rheims version). In Titus 2:13 we are urged to be *'looking for his appearing'*, i.e., the blazing forth of the glory of the *'man Christ Jesus'* as the One in whom *'dwelleth all the fullness of the Godhead bodily'* (Col. 2:9).

The Lord Himself described the day of his revealing, or of his *'appearing'*, if you will, in Luke 17:24, saying *'For just as the lightning flashes and lights up the sky from one end to the other, so will be the Son of Man in His day'*.

You see, it is the revealing of Christ as the great God Almighty and our Saviour (Titus 2:13) in blazing light that is *'our blessed hope'*. Why? Because the revealing, or *'appearing'* of Christ, as the *'great*

God' that He is, ushers in the day of Christ in which He will *'judge the quick and the dead'*.

This is when He will determine who should be resurrected to live with Him in his kingdom here on earth. It is also the time of our full salvation when we shall be presented faultless and unblameable before Him (1 Cor. 1:8, Jude 24, Col. 1:22). Meanwhile, we have been given every spiritual gift necessary to 'keep us on our toes' eagerly anticipating his appearing in the fullness of his glory.

Saving our spirit in the day of Christ

Now, without doubt, the next *'day of Christ'* scripture, **1 Cor. 5:5,** ranks as one of the hardest for a present-day Christian to believe. For it cuts across what many of us would hold dear. The very thought of a church meeting to condemn a fornicator to have his *'flesh'* destroyed by the devil sounds like something out of the dark days of the Roman Catholic Inquisition. Yet, actually it is good news, for it teaches there is salvation in the day of Christ from even the worst of sins.

1 Cor. 5:4-5 says:

> *…to deliver such a one to Satan for the destruction of the flesh that, that his spirit may be saved in the* **day of the Lord Jesus.** (NKJV)

What's more in 1 Cor. 5:3-4 the passage asserts that both Paul in his *'spirit'* and the Lord Jesus Christ in his *'power'* attended the meeting and agreed such sentence should be passed. One must ask, does the Apostle attend church meetings in his spirit today? Is the Lord Jesus present in *'power'* when elders meet today to pass judgement on the erring?

The answer is no and yes. No, the Apostle does not spiritually attend church disciplinary hearings today though his word is still with us. Yes, the Lord still does attend in his Spirit and again by the *'word of his power'*.

In 1 Cor. 5:5 there is an issue about whether the day mentioned there is the *'day of Christ'* or the *'day of the Lord'*. For while some Bibles have the wording *'the day of the Lord Jesus'* others have altered it to the 'day of the Lord'.

But what do the ancient texts in the Greek say? The Interlinear Bible reveals that in the Greek Received Text the words *'Kupiou Inoou'* are found, meaning the 'Lord Jesus', showing that it really should say *'in the day of the Lord Jesus'*.

To explain: The Received Text is the Greek Majority Text of the New Testament on which nearly all of the 5,000 ancient Bible manuscripts are founded. It has been accepted and loved as God's truth by believers around the world for nearly the last 2,000 years. Despite being translated into many languages the meaning of the Received Text has been so faithfully preserved, few significant differences can be found between manuscripts translated from it.

However, there are major variations in two other texts, the Codex Alexandra and the Codex Sinaiticus, which were rediscovered in the 19th century, and are considered corrupt by the best bible scholars. Nevertheless, their variations find their way into modern Bible translations with the result that in some references Christ's deity is omitted.

As to the meaning of the verse, the important truth is that even the spirit of a wicked man can be saved from sin in the *'day of Christ'*. And if that's true then there is hope that all people, or at least the vast majority of them, can be saved in this wonderful day.

It is important to realise that when this man was handed to Satan for the *'destruction of the flesh'* this did not imply destroying his actual body. The Roman Catholic inquisitors thought it did. Thus, they most cruelly tortured millions or burnt them to death. But, actually, the '*flesh*', is our sinful nature which the Lord through his apostle urges us to '*mortify*' or put to death, ourselves. Failure to do so can result in the Lord Himself disciplining and chastising us and in extreme cases handing us over to Satan for the destruction of the 'flesh', the sinful nature.

Salvation then is an ongoing work until it is gloriously completed in the '*day of Christ*'. However, where salvation means rescue from present evil it can be experienced in our lifetime on earth. Thus, in Phil. 1:19 Paul, speaking of his hoped-for release from prison, rejoices that his defence of the gospel '*...shall turn to my salvation through your prayer and the supply of the Spirit of Christ Jesus*'.

Rejoicing in Paul and Paul in us

Exultant joy by believers in the truth brought by Paul and in return Paul's joying in their faith is the theme of **2 Cor. 1:14**:

> *As also ye have acknowledged us in part that we are your rejoicing, even as ye are also ours in the day of the Lord Jesus.*

Yet, in sharp contrast, the only 'rejoicing' to be found in the day of the Lord is 1) by God-rejecting earth dwellers who kill the two prophets sent by God to torment them (Rev. 11:10), 2) by heaven dwellers at the casting down on the devil thus bringing woe to the earth (Rev. 12:12), and 3) when the holy prophets and apostles are told to rejoice at the prophesied destruction of Babylon (Rev. 18:20).

Significantly, there is no mention of joy or rejoicing in the scriptural passages which detail the coming '*day of the Lord*'.

Yet, in the '*day of Christ*' there will be joy over sinners fully saved and rejoicing that the gospel witness of redeemed believers during their days on earth has resulted in others also coming to Christ.

He which has begun a good work

Phil. 1:6, is a verse of great comfort. It tells us that not only will the Lord Jesus continually work to change us to be like Him throughout our present life but will also bring it to perfect completion in the *'day of Christ'*, that is, the life to come. However, the prospect of being changed into this glory is diminished if we fail to see the *'day of Christ'* as the great consummation of God's work of grace that it is.

That was the view hundreds of years ago of the noted Bible commentator, Matthew Henry, who, it seems, saw much that is missed by scholars of today. He wrote:

> The work of grace will never be perfected till the *'day of Jesus Christ'*, the day of his appearance. But we may always be confident God will perform his good work, in every soul wherein he has really begun it by regeneration; though we must not trust in outward appearances, nor in anything but a new creation to holiness.

The respected theologian Albert Barnes in his *Notes on the Bible*: comments that the day of Jesus Christ is:

> The day when Christ shall so manifest himself as to be the great attractive object, or the day when he shall appear to glorify himself, so that it may be said emphatically to be his day. It will be the day of his triumph and glory.

Thankfully, in Phil.1:6 all bibles agree that the reading is 'until the day of Christ', not the *'day of the Lord'*. The word 'until' is important. The Weymouth New Testament puts it well:

> *For of this I am confident, that He who has begun a good work within you will go on to perfect it in preparation for the day of Jesus Christ.*

Meaning, that come the *'day of Christ'* we will find ourselves perfect and unblameable before Him, not by our own efforts but by his working within us throughout our lives to change us into his image. But, please note, we will only be found so in *'the day of Christ'*, not at his return or so-called 'Second Coming' but when this great day of Christ begins with his *'appearing'*. Col. 3:4 mandates that …

> *…when Christ who is our life shall appear, then shall ye also appear with Him in glory.*

Rejoicing in the day of Christ

Our next verse, **Phil. 2:16,** confirms how good it will be for believers in the *'day of Christ'*. For this is when the Apostle Paul will rejoice and exult in the fact that he did not run in vain but that his ministry resulted in saving saints who then held out the *'word of Life'* to others in their life time.

> *Holding forth the word of life; that I may rejoice in the day of Christ that I have not run in vain, neither laboured in vain.*

In the Weymouth New Testament, Paul says: 'It will then be my glory on the day of Christ that I did not run my race in vain nor toil in vain'. In contrast to many translations which have Paul telling the Philippians to make sure they 'hold fast' to the 'Word of Life', The Amplified Bible also emphasises our need to share the gospel with others:

> *Holding out [to it] and offering [to all men] the Word of Life, so that in the Day of Christ I may have something of which exultantly to rejoice and glory in that I did not run my race in vain or spend my labour to no purpose.*

Allow me to ask a question of those who believe the *'day of Christ'* and the *'day of the Lord'* are one and the same: Would the

Apostle Paul rejoice in the '*day of the Lord*' when death and destruction is being rained on the earth and most of humanity destroyed? I think not. Not when he suffered so greatly to preach both the gospel of the kingdom and the gospel of grace the combination of which he describes as '*my gospel*' (1 Tim. 2:8) to the Gentile world.

You see, only in the '*day of Christ*' are believers fully saved and finally found blameless; only in that day will gospel preachers such as Paul see the full fruits of their labours.

To sum up, the day of Christ, as seen in references to it in Paul's epistles, is one of great blessing. It is when the spirits of even rebellious Christians, are saved, it is when our salvation becomes fully complete, it is when there is rejoicing over what we have done for the Lord. Above all, it is when Christ will be revealed in all his glory as the great God and Saviour and reward his saints. No wonder there will be great rejoicing then.

Chapter Eight - CAN WE FEEL GOD?

> Acts 17:25-27 - *God…giveth to all life, breath and all things and hath made of one blood all nations of men to dwell on all the face of the earth, and hath determined the times before appointed, and the bounds of their habitation … that they should* **seek** *the Lord, if haply they might* **feel** *after Him, and* **find** *Him though He be not far from every one of us. For in Him we live and move and have our being.*

Is it true you can feel God and know He is real? That is, can you receive a tangible manifestation of his presence? After all, isn't tangibly feeling God part of his glory? Surprisingly, both the Bible and the experience of millions of Christians say that the answer is 'yes'.

The issue is important because today some reject all or any notion of God because, they say, they cannot see, hear or touch Him. Therefore, they say, He is not real.

And once I was just such a person. Though brought up in a religious Christian home by the age of 30 I was an unsaved, hard-working, hard-drinking newspaperman, and a determined atheist.

Then God got on my case sending kindly relatives to tell me, amid the traumatic break-up of my first marriage, that I needed a Saviour and that the only one available was the Lord Jesus Christ. So, I went through the motions of repenting of sin and praying to receive Christ as the Saviour and Lord of my life. Then with a Bible under one arm I went to reconcile with my wife only to be rudely rebuffed for my pains. It was evident she didn't want to know the God who saves if meant making it up with me.

I then went to gospel rallies and emotional church meetings which advertised themselves as experiencing the 'real presence of God'. But to be honest I didn't feel a thing. What's more, depressed as I was, I felt totally out of place among those singing, clapping and waving their hands in the air with great enthusiasm. So after some months of this I went back to living in the world.

Fast forward three years and I still hadn't felt God but felt an inexplicable urge to visit my cousin Eileen and her husband George, who had earlier had travelled from Whangarei to Gisborne to tell me about the Lord and how to really encounter Him. Evidently God was still on my case. So as part of a holiday with my children and with a new lady in my life I drove from Wellington to Whangarei to see them.

It was there that all four of us committed ourselves to the Lord (in my case for the second time). I knew a big change was taking place inside me but I still hadn't felt or touched God. Nevertheless, it was noticeable my daughters were now happier than before.

It was on our way back and after stopping off to make peace with my parents (we had had an argument earlier) that I got a real 'touch from the Lord'. Heaven opened up and the glory of the Lord poured down upon me. The experience was so profound I lost all sense of my surroundings. Who drove the car for the next 70 kilometres, I do not know. I was not conscious of having a hand on the wheel and the others were asleep. Then after what must have been an hour I 'came to'. The car was safely stopped on the verge, the engine ticking over.

As the old chorus says, 'To get a touch from the Lord is so real'. And I got more than a touch. I got a baptism in the Lord's glory straight from heaven. And that sense of his presence has been a guide and comfort ever since. I treasure the times when the Lord makes

Himself real to me in a way I can feel. Fact is, if my heart is right toward God, then when I lift my hands to pray and worship Him, they tingle at his presence. I really feel it. It is a palpable, concrete experience. What's more his warmth comes into my heart as I open his book, the Bible, to study his word.

Does God want everyone to have this experience of glory? Undoubtedly, since He Himself says that the root problem with sin is that it causes '**all**' to *'come short of the glory of God'* (Rom. 3:23).

The glory God wants you to feel

Sadly, it seems many Christians fall short of this experience. In too many church services, the experience of the Lord is more cerebral than heart-felt and spiritual. Prayers are uttered and hymns are sung; there is a rational presentation of some Bible truths. But the sensation of the Lord being present is lacking. Indeed, some would discourage any such supernatural occurrence deeming it as excessive, over-enthusiastic, even dismissing it as carnal, a work of the flesh.

Yet, in Acts 17: 25-27, as quoted above, we are told that God has precisely placed the nations in their own lands with the express purpose that they might **seek** Him and **feel** after Him. Think of it. Each tribe and extended family of mankind has been given its own plot of earth on which to live and reach out to touch God. What's more He has already predetermined the '*times and bounds of their habitation'*, meaning that they are on probation, given only so long to feel and find God or to pass out of existence.

So, does God really want us to feel, to grope, after Him in order to really touch Him? Again, the answer is 'yes'. As the Apostle Paul said in effect in Acts 17: 27 we should so **seek** Him that we **feel** after Him and **find** Him. But does the Lord Himself want to be **felt** in that way? If we take his own word on the matter then, yes, He does. Did He not invite doubting Thomas to:

> '...reach hither thy finger and behold my hands, and reach hither thy hand and thrust it into my side and be not faithless but believing' (John 20:27)?

Remember, Thomas had said he would not believe the Lord had risen from the dead unless *'...I put my finger in the print of the nails and thrust my hand into his side'* (John 20:25). And you and I need to believe not only that Christ died for our sins but also that He rose from the dead and now lives as a life-giving, quickening spirit that we can feel.

Ps. 34: 8 says *'O taste and see that the Lord is good'*. Heb. 6:4 and 5 speaks of tasting the heavenly gift and the good word of God, and tasting means to touch with the tongue.

Consider also the testimony of the Apostle John who offered as proof that the risen Jesus is real and alive the fact that he and the other apostles had **'handled'** Him. Thus, 1 John 1:1 declares:

> *That which was from the beginning, which we have heard, which we have seen with our eyes, which we have looked upon, and our hands have handled of the Word of life.*

After his resurrection our Lord urged his eleven apostles to *'Behold my hands and my feet, that it is I myself: handle me and see, for a spirit hath not flesh and bones, as ye see me have'* (Luke 24:39). And in a way that is both spiritually and physically real He invites us today to come unto Him, to touch Him and be touched by Him.

It seems the Apostle Paul saw this touching and being touched by the Lord as the **quickening**. Thus in Eph. 2: 4-5 he writes:

> *But God who is rich in mercy, for his great love wherewith He loved us, even when we were dead in trespasses and sins hath* **quickened** *us together with Christ (by grace ye are saved).*

You see, God doesn't just sit and wait for us to seek and **feel** after Him; He makes it possible for us to feel and find Him by making us alive unto Him in our spirit even when we are sin-dead and don't want to know Him. We are like an unplugged radio but He switches us on and tunes us in to the sense of his presence and the reality of who He is. And that has tangible physical effects that can be really felt if, in response, we seek after Him and reach out to touch Him.

How real can that experience be? Well, in Matt. 9:20 speaking of our Lord's ministry on earth we are told of a woman who *'touched the hem of his garment'* believing that by doing so she would be *'made whole'* of a medically incurable haemorrhage. She touched Him and was healed.

Today we also can touch Him, feel him, and be *'made whole'* of our own incurable disease, that is our sin. And, as we touch his presence and believe, his blood (that is, his life now made spiritually and tangibly available to us) will wash us *'whiter than the snow'* (Ps. 51:7, Isa. 1:18). Why? Because He died on the cross taking our punishment for sin and now lives to give new life, his life, to all who will put their trust in Him (1 Cor. 15:3, Rom. 6:11).

Why don't you and I reach out afresh and touch Him for real today?

Chapter Nine -
A DIRECT EXPERIENCE OF HIS GLORY

It was as my former wife Marion lay dying at our home that Jesus appeared unto her in a sudden burst of his power and glory. Already the cold fingers of death had advanced upon her. Her limbs had lost all movement, her face had slumped and she hadn't spoke for hours. Now her arms and legs and even the top of her head were becoming still and cold.

Yet, suddenly, for a moment, life came back. Her face drew up again in the lovely smile that had caused me to fall in love with Marion years before. Her power to speak returned momentarily and still smiling with a loud voice she said 'Jesus', then slumped back in death as the presence of God filled the room and overwhelmed both her and me.

I had often wondered if the Lord really made Himself apparent at death to those who love Him and whose hope of life to come is fixed on Him. Now I knew the answer because Jesus had appeared to Marion at the time she needed Him most. I also knew without a shadow of doubt that Marion's soul and spirit were now safe in the arms of Jesus, secure in his keeping.

Earlier in the afternoon she had said goodbye to her son and daughter, giving her last testimony to them of her faith in Christ Jesus and the power of his resurrection. Marian's faith shone bright but her children chose not to stay as the end approached and left, leaving only me by her bedside.

We had been happily married for eleven years when she was diagnosed with an already advanced and aggressive form of bowel cancer. Various remedies were tried as we prayed asking the Lord to spare and heal her. It seemed a breakthrough when surgeons agreed to operate removing much of the affected bowel. But the cancer was spreading fast, wasting away Marion's body and sapping her energy to the point of exhaustion.

However, while her body was failing and doctors could offer only palliative care, Marion's faith and spirit rose high. She became a living embodiment of the truth the Apostle Paul wrote of in 2 Cor. 4:16: *'... though our outer man perish, yet the inward man is renewed day by day'.* Once an admittedly 'casual Christian' who as a teenager rebelled against her Salvation Army upbringing and married an unbeliever, Marion later became a Catholic, then worshipped in the Anglican Church on her journey of faith.

We met and married and in our last year together I was amazed to see Marion's faith and obedience to the Lord flourish. Her grasp of spiritual truth, as we realised the cancer was incurable and death was approaching, outstripped mine.

Marion took seriously 2 Cor. 4:14-15, the verses that precede the one quoted above. These state:

> *Knowing that He which raised up the Lord Jesus shall raise you up also by Jesus, and shall present us with you. For all things are for your sakes, that the abundant grace might through the thanksgiving of many redound to the glory of God.*

Together we majored on receiving and thanking God for his abundant grace. Marion declared this would be sufficient to see her through death to glory on the other side. Terribly weak after an operation, she left hospital wanting to be at home when the end came and set to planning her funeral down to the last detail. She then determined that in her last hours she would do what both Jesus and the martyr Stephen did before death. She committed her spirit into the hands of the Lord as a conscious act of faith.

Earlier, realising her cancer could not be cured, she had put her faith in the scripture, *'I can do all things through Christ who strengtheneth me'* (Phil. 4:13). So, despite being terribly weakened by a gruelling six-hour operation to remove the cancer-affected bowel, and then being dropped by a nurse who chose to save a drug administering apparatus rather than catching Marion as she fell, Marion was determined to get herself right with God. In particular, she took seriously Matt.10:32 in which Jesus says:

> *Whoever then will acknowledge Me before men, I will acknowledge him (or her) before my Father in heaven (NEB).*

A former Catholic for many years, confession became Marion's act of contrition. Not confession to a priest, that is, but confession by way of declaring to others her deeper found faith in Christ as her Saviour. She took to heart perhaps for the first time Rom. 10:9:

> *That if you confess with your mouth, Jesus is Lord and believe in your heart that God raised Him from the dead you will be saved (NIV).*

So, when in the recovery ward Marion went from bed to bed to share Christ and pray with other patients. This despite being ill and in pain herself. You see, for years going to church on Sunday and singing in the choir had largely constituted Christianity for Marion. The rest of the week was for work, dancing, shopping, chores and enjoying life. At that time confessing her faith in Christ to others, especially her own children, was not on her agenda. But all that changed in the lead up to her death.

In her last hours peace came upon her and at the end she found the strength to tell her children of their need to personally trust Jesus as their personal Saviour, something she had felt unable to do before.

Then, as death stole upon her, and she had long since lost the ability to speak, she did two amazing things.

Suddenly she lifted up her slumped face, smiled brilliantly and told me 'I love you', then fell back into decline. But a few minutes later she roused again and, this for the last time, lifting her face in greeting to cry 'Jesus!' The glory of his presence filled the room, then departed and her spirit left with Him.

When the Lord appears the second time

This was his **appearing** to her to welcome her home to be with Him. Up to then neither she nor I had understood the significance of the word **appearing** in scripture. But that night it became real to both of us.

It was only later I came to know that in Heb. 9:28 it is stated that Christ was *'…once offered to bear the sins of many* (i.e. at his first **appearing**) *and unto them that look for Him shall He* **appear the second time** *without sin unto salvation.*

You see the Lord had first **appeared** to Marion when she got saved. At that time, despite years of religious exposure, she knew no Saviour until Jesus became personally, tangibly real to her. Now He **appeared** to her again in the last hour of her life. But as I was to learn, and as this book seeks to explain, there was much more to learn about his **appearing**.

Meanwhile, if you are aware of your own approaching mortality and this story has touched your heart you might want to pray the following prayer:

Dear Lord, you teach me to know my days are numbered. Help me to cling solely to you as the hope of my resurrection and eternal life. As the end of my life approaches help me by your Spirit to commit my spirit into your hands. Help me to know my future lies wholly with you. Lord, please reveal your glory to me.

Chapter Ten - EMPOWERED BY HIS GLORY NOW

As far as we know the Apostle Paul never met the saints at Colossi, nor those at Laodicea (Col. 2:1). But he prayed a series of prayers for them that are among the most powerful found in scripture. Indeed, the whole epistle to the Colossians is full of how believers both then and now can receive and walk in the might of '*his* (that is Christ's) *glorious power*'.

The Apostle also desired that these believers who, like us, have never seen his face in the flesh (Col. 2:1) *'…might be filled with the knowledge of his will in all wisdom and spiritual understanding… that ye might walk worthy of the Lord unto all pleasing, being fruitful in every good work and increasing in the knowledge of God'* (Col. 1:9-10).

But it is verse 11 that we now focus on because here the apostle prays for believers to be:

> …strengthened with all **might** according to his (Christ's) **glorious power** unto all patience and longsuffering with joyfulness.

The **Interlinear Bible** translates the passage more strongly:

> …being **empowered** with all **power** according to the **might** of his (Christ's) **glory** to all patience and longsuffering with joy.

The **New Heart English Bible** says:

> …strengthened with all power, according to the **might of his glory**, for all endurance and perseverance with joy.

The **Aramaic Bible in Plain English** states:

> *And that you would be empowered with all strength according to the **majesty of his glory,** with all patience, endurance and joy.*

Clearly then the **power** of Christ lies in his glory and his glory is that of his **majesty**, the position God has set Him in as the king of heaven and earth and '*and put all things under his feet and gave Him to be Head over all things to the church*' (Eph. 1:22). And Paul is praying that believers who have never seen his face (and that includes us) may receive this power of Christ's glory now.

There is no reason to believe that God did not hear the apostle's prayer and answer it, nor that his plea for those who love Christ to be empowered with his might was not granted. But there is a problem. Paul himself writing to the same Colossians in the same letter says: '*Ye are dead*' and the Lord and our (future) life with Him are at present '*hid in God*' (Col. 3:3). He then states (Col. 3:4):

> *When Christ who is our life shall **appear** then shall ye also **appear** with Him in glory.*

Question: If the full glory of Christ – always God but once made a man to die for our sins, and now a man declared to be God in glory - is yet to appear, then how come we as believers can receive the **power** of this glory now? Answer: by way of a special dispensation of God's grace thanks to the prayer of Paul. Remember that Paul was the last of the apostles to see the Lord but he saw Him as '*one born out of due time*' (1 Cor. 15:8).

Simply put, '*out of due time*' means that while the other apostles saw the resurrected Jesus **before** his ascension, Paul saw him **after** his ascension and indeed saw Him as the glorified Lord. In fact Jesus, now having been given '*all power in heaven in earth*' (Matt. 28:18), **appeared** unto Paul, then Saul, his arch-enemy on earth, in such a blaze of glory from heaven it outshone the midday sun (Acts 26:13).

Now, when Christ eventually **appears** to all the world in in his full glory as King of kings and Lord of lords (1 Tim. 6: 14-16) the light will be even stronger. It will be light '*that no man can approach unto*' for when our Lord is revealed at this time it will be in *'the fullness of the Godhead bodily'* (Col. 2:9). And we are told that his **appearing** (Col. 3:4, Titus 2:13, 1 Tim. 6:14) is our *'blessed hope'* that we should be earnestly seeking and looking for.

And if all that is so, how is it that we can have a foretaste, a real experience of the power of his glory right now, even before the 'due time' for the manifestation of his kingdom at his **appearing** (2 Tim. 4:1)? The answer, in my view, can be found in two words: God's grace. For in the grace of God provision is made for the power of God.

More power than you can imagine

Today then believers saved by grace are truly empowered by God Himself with power that really works. God's Word says so. Rom. 1:16 states that the *'gospel of Christ is the **power** of God unto salvation to everyone that believeth'*. Please note, it says 'is', not 'was', meaning that this power is for today. This gospel of grace has enough power to save everyone on the planet should they believe but God promises even more power to those who trust His Word.

For example, in Eph. 1:19 Paul the Apostle to the Gentiles speaks of the *'exceeding greatness of His* (God's) ***power** to us who believe'*. Think about it. He is saying that however 'great' you imagine God's power is toward us believers, in fact it is far, far greater. We know that is true because in Eph. 3:20 we learn that God the Father is *'able to do exceedingly abundantly above all that we ask or think'* – and look out, here it comes – *'according to the **power** that works within us.'*

Believer, God says you've got more **power** at work in you than you could ever imagine, pray for or dream about. What's more both

God the Father and the Apostle Paul want you to try it out – to see how it works through you and for you – just so that you know how great that **power** is within you. Thus in Eph. 1:17 Paul prays:

> *That the God of our Lord Jesus Christ, the Father of glory may give unto you the spirit of wisdom and revelation in the knowledge of Him (the Father): The eyes of your understanding being enlightened: that ye may know what is the hope of his calling and what the riches of the glory of his inheritance in the saints.*
>
> *And what is the exceeding greatness of his **power**, which He wrought in Christ when He raised Him from the dead and set Him at His own right hand in the heavenly places,*
>
> *Far above all principality, might and dominion and every name that is named, not only in this world but in the world which is to come. And hath put all things under His feet and gave Him to be Head over all things to the Church which is His Body, the fullness of Him that filleth all in all.*

Do you see how this **power** works? In answer to the Apostle Paul's prayer the Father Himself gives us the spirit of wisdom and revelation in the knowledge of Him – Him being the Father Himself but revealed only through the Son. The result of that prayer is that the *'eyes of your understanding'* are opened so you can know **three** things:

1. The **hope** of his calling.

2. The **riches** of the glory of his (that is, God's) inheritance in the saints.

3. The exceeding greatness of his **power** to usward who believe.

And that's not all. This **power** that is **exceeding great** is *'according to the working of **his mighty power**'.* Note well, this is not just God's **power** at work. That would be stupendous enough but this is God's **mighty power** at work **in us** who believe.

And even that is not all. Actually, this **mighty power** of God is at work in us in the same way it worked back when God exerted more of his **power** than on any other occasion we know of from Scripture. That, of course, was when He raised His precious Son Jesus Christ from the death which He died when He bore our sin on the cross. You see, however much **power** it took to create the heavens and the earth – and that was heaps – it took much more to raise Christ from His death for our sin. It is this **exceeding great power** that God wants you and me to know as a real experience in our lives.

Look, how much spiritual **power** do you personally need to live for and love the Lord? However much it is God has more. More **power** than the supposed Big Bang scientists falsely claim exploded the universe into being. Far more bang in fact than a billion supernovae exploding at once. And that exceeding great **power** needs to be as powerful as that because it is the very **power** of the new creation (for which see Matt. 19:28 [regeneration] and Acts 3:21 [restitution]). Yes, believer, it takes much more of God's **power** to conform us to the image of God's son (Rom. 8:29) and make us a new creature in Christ (2 Cor. 5:17) than it did to bring a billion stars unto being.

This **power** raised Christ when He had been crushed to death by our sin and God's punishment for it that He took on our behalf. From death God the Father's **mighty power** lifted Him high into the heavenlies. Then this **power** placed Him higher still, far above all principality, power, might and any name in either this world or the world to come (Eph. 1:21-22).

This means any evil power that is in you or comes against you when you seek to do God's will is powerless to prevent, alter or hinder anything God through His **mighty power** does in your life. This **power** has also made Him Head over all things to us, His Church. No wonder Paul says: *'We are more than conquerors through Him that loved us'* (Rom. 8:37).

It is through this **power**, flowing from the death, burial and resurrection of Jesus Christ that we have been made alive. What's more we have Christ Himself alive in us *'the hope of glory'*, the inner man who cannot sin. However, as Paul says, we have this *'treasure in earthen vessels, so that the excellency of the* **power** *may be of God and not of us*' (2 Cor. 4:7).

Do you get it? There is more enough **power** from God to give us hope (and in the Bible that means *'certainty'*, see Heb. 6:11) that we will arrive in glory. However, the **power**, like the **glory**, must be of God and not of us. It must also be of love since love covers a multitude of sins (1 Peter 4:8). And it is, and it does.

Amazing grace, isn't it? And yet, perhaps, like me, you sometimes feel all this is a little too good to be true? After all, here I am, still a sinner, still struggling with some aspects of life, not to mention having difficulty achieving godliness. Why is it when so much of God's **power** is available, we sometimes feel very defeated by sin and Satan, rather than rejoicing in the scriptural fact that that in Christ we are *'more than conquerors'* (Rom. 8:37)?

Ah, perhaps like me, you're a 'special case', one that struggles with sin, one that needs further empowering to see all that God has done and is doing for you. If so, then I have good news for you. You see, amazingly, God's word offers even **more** of God's **power** to meet the need in such a case.

Power flowing from the inner man

That's right, there's further **power** over and above all that we've talked about thus far and it's there especially to meet the needs of poor sinners such as you and I. To find it we go to Eph. 3:14-16. Here Paul writes:

> *For this cause, I bow my knees unto the Father of our Lord Jesus Christ, of whom the whole family in earth and heaven is named, that He would grant you, according to the riches of His glory, to be* **strengthened** *with* **might** *by his Spirit in the* **inner man***: That Christ may dwell in your hearts by faith ...*

Here are some weak believers. Yes, they are saved. Yes, they have been baptised by God's Spirit into His (Christ's) Body. They've experienced God the Father's saving and raising power and, yes, they have each put on the *'new man'* (Eph. 4:24) who is holy – that man who is, in fact, Christ Himself dwelling by his Spirit within us.

But they need strengthening to stand in the battle for truth – don't we all? That is precisely why Paul asks the Father to strengthen us with **might** by his Spirit in the inner man.

You see the Apostle knows who he is ministering to, i.e., us Gentiles. He knows what we are like. He knows, and God knows, we can receive the benefits of the wonderful *'gospel of the grace of God'* (Acts 20:24), yet still fail to *'grow up into Him in all things'* (Eph. 4:15).

Why is it we don't fully grow up as we should? Answer: Because we are weak. Paul found the solution to this problem was not to pretend to be strong but to admit he was weak. Christ told Paul, *'My strength is made perfect in weakness'* (2 Cor. 12:9). Paul's response was: *'Most gladly therefore will I glory in my infirmities (*weaknesses*) that the* **power** *of Christ may rest on me'*.

Now, here in Eph.3:14-16 Paul prays that we weak believers may strengthened with the Father's **might** in the inner man. We really do need strengthening with that special **power** of God, his **exceeding great might**. And where do we need strengthening? Not in our flesh but, oddly enough, right in the **inner man** where you might think such **power** was needed least, since the inner *'hidden man of the heart'* (1 Pet. 3:4) is said to be holy and righteous.

Ah, but it is precisely in our outworking (working out) of that inner man, through our daily thoughts and deeds, that we Gentiles have such difficulty. This is why God, speaking through the Apostle Paul, knows and prescribes what is best for us – strengthening with His **might** in the inner man. Our inner man must become stronger, not in and of himself - he doesn't need to – but in the effect, he has upon and in our lives.

This is why Paul prays especially prays for you and for me, grace-saved believers, that we might be strengthened with **might** by God's Spirit in the inner man. So, let's be weak that we may be strong and let his power flow in love to us through his Son.

Chapter Eleven - IS THE TABERNACLE OF DAVID A KEY?

> Amos 9:11 - *In that day I will raise up the Tabernacle of David that is fallen and close up the breaches thereof; and I will raise up his ruins, and I will build it as in the days of old.*
>
> Acts 15:13-18 - *And after they had held their peace James answered, saying, Men and brethren, hearken unto me: Simeon hath declared how God at the first did visit the Gentiles to take out of them a people for his name.*
>
> *And to this agree the words of the prophets: As it is written, after this, I will return and will build again the Tabernacle of David, which is fallen down; and I will build again the ruins thereof, and I will set it up:*
>
> *That the residue of men might seek after the Lord and all the Gentiles, upon whom my name is called, saith the Lord who doeth all these things. Known unto God are all his works from the beginning of the world.*

Is COVID19 and Russia's invasion of the Ukraine but the prelude to a series of further disasters set to strike the world? Strong evidence suggests it may be so. For example, Australia is having to import wheat for the first time in 12 years, as a result of drought-ruined harvests and, according to the *New Scientist*, Africa Swine Disease (AFD) has destroyed half of China's pigs and killed a quarter of pigs worldwide. Meanwhile, billions of tonnes of needed crops have been ploughed under unbought for lack of means to transport them.

So, already hunger is stalking the earth. UN World Food Programme head David Beasley recently warned that starvation is rapidly rising heading the world into the 'worst humanitarian crisis since World War II'. Short of dramatic intervention, 300,000 people a day will starve to death, he predicts. And if you think we in the West won't be affected, then know that already Wendy's, fearing a meat shortage, has taken burgers off-menu in a fifth of its restaurants. Indeed, food supplies are shrinking worldwide in the face of a 'perfect storm' that combines awful droughts in Africa with swarms of locusts the size of cities eating everything in their path elsewhere.

Economically, the world is facing a massive downturn that could last for decades. Already airlines, tourism, and a host of other industries worldwide are in jeopardy; their revenues slashed, their pricing now prohibitive and their recovery highly doubtful. Experts say that already COVID19 has produced the worst economic slump in Britain since the days of King Charles I, if not that of 1207AD. Not only are these damaging effects all but unprecedented. Troubles are coming one on top of another in an accelerating chain of events that begets further disaster.

However, while some are now asserting that through this God is judging the world, giving mankind a sharp wake-up call ahead of the 'rapture' and his return, this writer takes a different view. He believes man himself is to blame for these successive calamities, not God; that we are reaping what we have sown.

Thus, COVID19 and its consequences plus the Russian invasion of the Ukraine, are not a punishment from God but add urgency to his call for all men to be reconciled unto Him and receive the free forgiveness made available by Christ's death for our sin. Now then, God is still acting as the *'God of all grace'* in this, the *'dispensation of the grace of God'* (Eph. 3:1-4).

Nevertheless, the dark trouble now stalking the earth may well be setting the stage for the next great move of God – his **appearing** and the bringing in of the **kingdom of heaven on earth** that Jesus promised would occur and told us to pray for.

And one key to grasping this wonderful prospect is a better understanding of the prophecies about the **Tabernacle of David**. Sadly, to date dispensationalists have taken a too narrow approach to understanding God's 'Plan of the Ages' from scripture. In largely setting Israel aside they have concentrated on the dispensational truths of the Pauline revelation for Gentiles at the expense of the Hebrew prophetic promises that are also needed to complete the picture.

In doing so, for example, they have ignored the sequence of events outlined in James' Acts 15:16 prophecy about the Tabernacle of David. But they are not alone. Christendom at large has also ignored this important teaching just as it has overlooked the important truth of Acts 3:21, which declares Jesus must remain in heaven until the *'times of the restitution of all things'* are completed.

This latter crucial pronouncement by the Apostle Peter means that neither the 'rapture' nor the Lord's return to earth can occur until the wonderful era of God restoring the earth to its pre-Flood beauty and bringing mankind back to Himself is completed first.

And it is the Tabernacle of David that provides the timeline for when this glorious day of recreation will be brought in. However, before going further allow me to ask a few questions about the present situation and what it means.

Has the Lord returned yet? No. Has He already rebuilt the Tabernacle of David? No. Is it significant that the current COVID19 pandemic has shut church doors and stopped services around the globe? Yes. Could the resultant economic downturn be the prelude to the Lord revealing Himself in glory? My hope is that it will be.

Now, it has been rightly said by another that the inspired words of James about David's Tabernacle in Acts 15:13-18 set out with 'clearness, brevity and eloquence' the plan of God for this age in which we live. Trouble is that few, if any of us, have seen this as the key to understanding what God has already done, is doing now, and will shortly do in our time.

Actually, there are three steps to this great plan and purpose as set out by James in Acts 15. They are:

> FIRST: **Visiting** the Gentiles 'to **take out of them a people for his name**' (vs 14). I.e., the '*few that be saved*' (Luke 13:23ff.) in the present dispensation.

> SECOND: '**After this**', '**I will return** and build again '*the Tabernacle of David which is fallen down*' (vs. 16). This so that:

> THIRD: '… *the residue of men*' (i.e., **all** the unsaved and **all** the Gentiles (actually the word is *ethnos* meaning 'nations') not yet saved might '***seek after the Lord*** and thus also be saved.

So, the key phrases that spell out God's timetable for saving us and then the world are:

1. **Visiting the Gentiles**
2. **To take out a people for his name**
3. **After this**
4. **I will return**
5. **And build again the Tabernacle of David**
6. **Which is fallen down**
7. **That the residue of men might seek after the Lord and all the Gentiles, upon whom my name is called, saith the Lord:**

Let's look at these seven stages in more detail.

1) **Visiting the Gentiles:** We see that the Lord speaking through James says that *'after this, I will return'* (Acts 15:16). **After** what one might ask? The answer is **after** *'God did visit the Gentiles to take out of them a people for his name'* (Acts 15:14). This visitation began with Simon Peter's preaching the gospel to the Gentile house of Cornelius the Roman centurion in Acts 10, was then continued by Paul and is still taking place today.

   Thus, it is seen that it is not until this preaching of salvation to the Gentiles, indeed to the whole world, is completed that God takes the next step of rebuilding the Tabernacle of David.

   Elsewhere in scripture, this dispensation of God is called *'the times of the Gentiles'*. Jesus said Jerusalem would be *'trodden down of the Gentiles'* until these times were fulfilled (Luke 21:24). Importantly, being saved under this, the still current stage of salvation, is for individuals. God is not now saving nations as such, still less the world as a whole. As Rom. 10:13 summarises: *'Whomsoever shall call, upon the name of the Lord shall be saved'*. God is now saving people one by one.

2) **To take out a people for his name:** What a mistake it has been to believe that it is God's present purpose to save the whole world. For 2,000 years colossal efforts have been poured into missions at home and abroad and, huge amounts of money have been spent to achieve, at best, only a minority truly saved here or there. For sure, it is God's purpose ultimately to save all people, but not now, only later.

Before the Lord brings about global salvation for all people it seems He must first call, save and select a company of dedicated individual disciples willing to suffer in this life in order to '*rule and reign*' with Him in the next. Thus, the challenge now to every Christian is to be found worthy to bear his name.

As the Apostle Paul said: '*... if we be dead with Him we shall also live with Him; if we suffer, we shall also reign with Him*' (2 Tim. 2:11-12). God's present purpose then is to save and select '*a little flock*' of the Gentiles, taken out of all '*nations*', including some Jewish people, all of whom will be, and are being, '*made conformable unto his death*' (Phil. 3:10).

In the reinstated Tabernacle of David these proven disciples will join the called out '*remnant*' from Israel to shine with the Lord in glory when He makes his **appearing** (Col. 3:1-4).

3) **After this I will return:** Note that it is only **after this** calling out of a selected company of people from the Gentiles (i.e., the nations) that the Lord Almighty says '**I will return**'. The Lord will not **return**, will not **appear**, still less come again, until this present purpose of his is accomplished.

And this purpose of His will not be completed '*...until the fullness of the Gentiles be come in*' (Rom. 11:25). As already stated, many of us have mistakenly thought it is God's purpose to save the whole world now, in our time.

Indeed, vast efforts have been made by churches, organisations and individuals to 'win the world for Christ'. After all, didn't Christ say that '*I, if I be lifted up, I will draw all men unto Me*'? Wasn't He sent to be the '*Saviour of the world*'? (John 4:42 and 1 John 4:14) Yes, He was, and He will be, but later not now.

4) **And build again the Tabernacle of David:** Please note it is the Lord Himself who will rebuild this fallen down tabernacle. He says: '*I will build again the ruins thereof and I will set it up*'. Its re-establishment will be accomplished only by the '*the Lord who doeth all these things*'.

I say that because for more than 60 years well-meaning Pentecostals and Charismatics have held that their music, singing, and worship is actually rebuilding David's Tabernacle. It is not. Now granted, it is wonderful and right to enter God's courts with praise and sense his presence through thankfulness and worship. For, the Father seeks those who will '*worship Him in spirit and in truth*'.

However, it must be re-iterated that since God is **not** now restoring the Tabernacle of David, such commendable worship is not rebuilding the Tabernacle of David. Only God can do that and He will do so only in time to come. That 'time' is denoted by James' inspired statement, '**After this…**' It is also important to realise there was much more to David's Tabernacle than extravagant worship, beautiful though that was and is.

5) **Which is fallen down:** Note carefully the tense employed here. James did not say the tabernacle **had** fallen down. He said it '*is fallen down*'. In other words, the Tabernacle of David was something of God that, spiritually speaking,

should have continued with Israel from the time of its erection and certainly should have been operating in the Book of Acts period when James uttered these words.

That it did not is evidenced by the fact Israel had so ceased meaningful outreach to Gentiles, not only in Old Testament times but also in the Acts period, that God set them aside as a nation and '*sent salvation to the Gentiles*' in Acts 28:28. Thus ended Israel's days as the sole means and 'bringer of salvation'.

Her essential purpose in God had been to '*bless all nations*' and to be '*a light of the Gentiles, that thou shouldest be for salvation unto the ends of the earth*' (Acts 13:47). But this the chosen nation refused to do and thus the Tabernacle of David became '*fallen down*'.

However, God is going to raise it up again. But not just yet. First, He has purposed to take out of all nations a people for his name and that is what He has been doing for the last 2,000 years and is still doing to this day. It is, however, a selective salvation. Though all are called, not all are saved. And not all those saved '*press toward the prize of the high calling of God in Christ Jesus*' (Phil. 3:14).

But just as Jesus chose 12 disciples as apostles to minister with and for Him (Luke 6:13), so God is now taking out a special people so that He can rebuild the Tabernacle of David with them as his servants. This specially chosen, tried and tested company will appear with Him at his **appearing** (Col. 3:1-4) which is the blazing forth of his glory (Titus 2:13).

Thus, Christ will appear in his fullness as the resurrected man now fully glorified as God but also glorified in that the glorified saints appear with Him as his *'body'*. This so that all the world may be saved through his and their witness.

Online author J. Preston Eby sheds light on this, asserting that far from being a physical tent the Tabernacle of David will be the company of saved, sanctified, and manifested sons of God that Rom. 8:18-24 says will deliver all creation into the *'glorious liberty of the Son of God'*. This is the great and glorious event all creation longs for.

It is the time when Adam's curse of sin and death will be lifted, when the glory of the Lord shall fill the earth as the waters cover the sea, when the Lord will bring in the kingdom of heaven to rule over the earth, when man will be set free from sickness and sin and when the Lord Jesus Christ will appear in his full glory as the Man who is God (Titus 2:13, 1 Tim. 6: 14-16).

It is the time the Apostle Paul called the *'day of Christ'* seven times in his epistles to believers of this age. It is the **'appearing'** (*epiphanea*) both he and the Apostle Peter spoke of as *'the **appearing** of Jesus Christ'* (1 Pet. 1:7, Titus 2:13 and 2 Tim. 4:8). It is the wonderful day in which the Lord will *'judge the quick and the dead at his **appearing** and his kingdom'* (2 Tim. 4:1).

6) **That the residue of men might seek after the Lord and all the Gentiles** (i.e., nations), **upon whom my name is called, saith the Lord:** Note the contrast here. Hitherto God has been taking out a selected company of Gentiles and Jews largely individual by individual. No nations

have been saved as such. But in the *'day of Christ'* when the Tabernacle of David is restored and is revealed, replete with a chosen company of people, *'all the nations'* will be saved, not one by one but collectively *en masse* as nations. As the Psalmist wrote in Ps. 72: 8 and 11:

He (the glorified, revealed Christ) *shall have dominion from sea to sea and from the river to the ends of the earth. Yea, all kings shall fall down before Him: all nations shall serve Him.*

Ps. 22:27 - *All the ends of the earth shall remember and turn unto the Lord: and all the kindreds of the nations shall worship before Thee.*

Prayer:

Thank you, Lord, that you still want to save the world and its people. Thank you that you have called us as believers to be part with you in this great and holy enterprise. Help us to see how important your purpose is in this and by your grace prepare and equip us for the task ahead. In Jesus' mighty name we pray.

Chapter Twelve - THE FINGER OF GOD

> Luke 11:20 - *But if I with the **finger of God** cast out devils, no doubt the **kingdom of God** is come upon you.*
>
> Luke 5:17 - *And it came to pass on a certain day that that there were Pharisees and doctors of the law sitting by, which were come out of every town of Galilee, and Judea, and Jerusalem, and the **power of the Lord was present** to heal them.*
>
> Exodus 8:19 - *Then the magicians said unto Pharoah, This is the **finger of God**: and Pharoah's heart was hardened and he hearkened not unto them; as the Lord had said.*
>
> 2 Timothy 3:5,8,9 - *Having a form of godliness but **lacking the power thereof**; from such turn away. Now as Jannes and Jambres withstood Moses, so do these also resist the truth: men of corrupt minds, reprobate concerning the faith. But they shall proceed no further: for their folly shall be manifest unto all men, as theirs was also.*

What a wonderful thing it is when God does something in your life and you know it's from God and from no one else and through no one else. It's a first-hand, not second-hand, experience. It is the **finger of God** at work in and upon you. Importantly, when you are touched by the Lord's finger you know it is Him and not another; you recognise this by both his presence and his power.

I am convinced not only that the **finger of God** can come to each true believer to cast out fear, evict devils, heal, restore and provide whatever may be lacking but that at certain times it actually does…

Fact is, there is no effective substitute for experiencing God one on one. Unless it is He personally that acts, unless it is his **finger** that writes upon *'the fleshy tables of our heart'* and his voice that we hear, we are left with the *'dry bones'* of a second-hand experience passed on by somebody else. And, while the testimony of others may be encouraging it is not the same as a direct encounter with God Himself. After all, isn't that how we first got saved – by a direct encounter with the living Saviour, the Lord Jesus Christ?

It's the same when we seek help. Unless it is the touch of his hand we feel when prayed for our petitions go mainly unanswered. 'To get a touch from the Lord is so real', the old chorus says. But in today's largely powerless but strongly religious Christendom the song might well have said, 'To get a touch from the Lord is so rare'.

Millions cry out for God to make Himself real to them. Some flock to meetings where some men and women, who claim to able to physically heal folk and deliver them from devils, put themselves forward as intermediaries between those seeking deliverance and the Lord Himself. In such emotionally charged meetings few stop to consider 1 Tim. 2:5 which categorically states: *For there is one God and mediator between God and men, the man Christ Jesus.* Others need not apply to be a mediator. However, they can reflect the Lord's glory and effect an introduction.

Today faced with crisis, business bankruptcy and likely world economic collapse, thanks to war and COVID19, there is more need now to experience that which only God can do than at any previous time in our lifetimes. And I am convinced that *'our great God and Saviour Jesus Christ'* (Titus 2:13) stands poised once again to write in a new better world with his finger, **the finger of God.** Let us see why.

In scripture we find that the **finger of God** appears in times of danger and dire need. For example, it was when Moses withstood the magicians at Pharoah's court that the **finger of God** did something the Egyptian wizards could not do – turn the dust of the earth into lice. Hitherto the magicians had duplicated every miracle through their enchantments, turning rods into snakes and water into blood. But they could not imitate what the finger of God could do.

Later, it seemed that only Jesus and his appointed apostles could cast out devils by the **finger of God.** (Luke 11:20) For when the sons of a Jewish priest tried to do so at Ephesus, the demon they tried to evict sent them fleeing, bruised and naked. (Acts 19:14-16)

If scripture is to be believed then real healing and deliverance happen only when God Himself or his appointed representatives turn up to perform these tasks. Thus, in Luke 5:17 it was only because *'the power of the Lord was present to heal'* that the man with palsy was restored to health.

A promise for all time

Today the big question is: Will the **finger of God** move for us in this, our time of need? Or will we be left to seek succour from so-called miracle workers who promise much and deliver little? I would suggest, that if scripture is allowed to have a say, that God will indeed expose the claims of those who have *'a form of godliness but lacking the power thereof,'* (2 Tim. 3:5) by pointing his **finger** at them.

In 2 Tim. 3:5, 8 and 9 the Apostle Paul explains how this will happen. Speaking specifically of those who *'have a form of godliness but lacking the power thereof,'* he says: *'But they shall proceed no further: for their folly shall be manifest unto all men, as theirs* (that of the Egyptian magicians Jannes and Jambres) *was also'.*

The order of such divine intervention is clear. Those *'lacking the power thereof'* are shown up for the *'clouds without water'* (Jude 12) that they really are when God appears and with his finger does the real miracles they cannot perform. However, He does so in his way and in his time.

So, what promise do we have that the Lord will intervene for us with his **finger** and power, living as we do in *'this present evil world'* (Gal. 1:4) which is run by the *'prince of the power of the air'* (Eph. 2: 2)?

Many have tried to activate the promises of manifest divine power vouchsafed in the time of the gospel accounts or that of Acts. But, in too many cases, attempts today to replicate such miracles of the past meet with failure. Devils 'cast out in Jesus' name' often refuse to depart or return a day or so later. Some healings stubbornly do not take place and prayers to see souls saved often see no such result in the short term.

But there is a key that applies in every age or dispensation. A promise that holds good for all time. It concerns the kingdom of God, or the kingdom of heaven as it is also termed in scripture. Notice that in Luke 11:20 Jesus said that when He cast out devils by the **finger of God** then the kingdom of God had come upon those witnessing such miracles:

> *But if I with the finger of God cast out devils, no doubt the kingdom of God is come upon you.*

It is the power brought to bear by this intervention of the kingdom, ahead of the designated time for its full prophetic fulfilment that we need. Remember that Jesus told his disciples to *'seek first the kingdom of God'* (Matt. 6:33).

It is this advance *'earnest'* or down payment of this kingdom's power that Paul was talking about when he said to *'turn away'* from those lacking it. (2 Tim. 3:5). It is also the *'exceeding greatness of his* (God's) *power'* (Eph.1:19) that the apostle prayed for us to know and personally experience.

What's more in Heb. 6:4 the Apostle says believers in his lifetime had:

> *…been enlightened, tasted of the heavenly gift, and have been made partakers of the Holy Spirit, and have tasted the good word of God and the powers of the age to come…*

It may have been a 'taste' but it was a good taste. It was an *'earnest'*, a 'deposit' through the Spirit of Christ of what is to come (Eph. 1:13-14). But God doesn't want us to be satisfied with a mere 'taste'. He wants us to be looking for the four or eight course meal we will get in in the '*day of Christ'*.

But, you might ask, how do we tap into such a marvellous resource – a power which is said to be *'to usward'* (Eph. 1:19)*?* I am firmly convinced we can do so by obeying the commandment of the Lord Jesus Christ given through the Apostle through Paul in Titus 2:13 that we should be:

> *…looking for that blessed hope and the glorious **appearing** of our great God and Saviour Jesus Christ.*

Why should we do so? Because in 2 Tim. 4:1 we are told that Christ will *'… judge the quick and the dead at his **appearing** and his **kingdom'**.* The two are almost synonymous in that it is at his **appearing** that He will bring in the **kingdom** of heaven on earth by taking over government of this world in a blaze of glory.

The result will be the ushering in of arguably the most blessed period of all in human history. Sin, death, sickness and war will be banished. Every eye will be turned to the Lord. His glory will shine 24/7 and peace and prosperity will be the hallmark of his reign. Best of all the **finger of God** will be at work all the time because where the King (Jesus) is, so is his kingdom, power and glory. And the **finger of God** will be the ever-present evidence of it.

As scripture teaches (Ex. 8:19 and 2 Tim. 3:9), it is when the forces of darkness seem to triumph – as they seem to be doing right now in this sad and dying world of ours – that our Saviour, the God Almighty, the Lord Jesus Christ reaches out to touch both us and our situation with the very **finger of God.**

Chapter Thirteen - GENTILE BLESSINGS IN THE DAY OF CHRIST

(This three-part study was written in 2013 but was quickened afresh to me by the Lord as an important summary of the soon-to-be Day of Christ).

Part One

> Isaiah 42:1 - *Behold my servant whom I uphold: mine elect in whom my soul delighteth: I have put my spirit upon Him;* **he shall bring forth judgment to the Gentiles.**
>
> Isaiah 49:6 - *And He said, It is a light thing that thou shouldest be my servant to raise up the tribes of Jacob and restore the preserved of Israel: I will also give thee for a* **light to the Gentiles** *that thou mayest be my salvation unto the ends of the earth.*
>
> Isaiah 66:18 - *… It shall come, that I will gather* **all nations and tongues** *and they shall come and see* **my glory**.

We live in the dispensation of the grace of God and today God's ministry is toward Gentiles, indeed to everybody, for in Eph. 3:1-2 the word for Gentiles is *ethnos* meaning 'nations'. And grace would teach us that tomorrow in the *'day of Christ'* (Phil. 1:6, 2:16). Gentiles (all nations) will still be the first to benefits from the '*times of refreshing'* (Acts 3:19).

As seen from the verses above it is a scriptural fact that Gentiles on earth in that day will receive their greatest blessings thus far from the hand of God. And the Gentiles, indeed all men, will receive blessings first before the Lord sets His hand to redeem and restore Israel.

This is why Isa. 42:1 uncompromisingly proclaims that God's servant *'... shall bring forth judgment to the **Gentiles**.'* And why Isa. 49:6 says the servant will be a light to the Gentiles and God's salvation to the ends of the earth. It is also why in Isa. 66:18 it is all nations and tongues, not just Israel, that are gathered to see the glory of the Lord.

At first *'in that day'* Israel will not count as God's favoured nation, any more than it does so in God's eyes now. Prophecy makes clear that only the Israel that God redeems and restores to their ancient land will be counted by God as his Israel and, scripturally speaking, that hasn't happened yet.

So, in the *'day of Christ'* Gentiles will be first to receive the Lord's judgement and that's a good thing, because most Gentiles have so long been trodden down by oppressive spiritual forces they no longer know what true judgement is. Mention the word and immediately it prompts a picture of a judge dealing out harsh punishment. But that is not what is meant by judgement in Isa. 42:1.

Rather it's a matter of 'putting things right'. A New Zealand businessman built his large appliance dealership on just those words. His slogan was: 'It's the putting right that counts'. And 'putting it right' is exactly what judgement means in Isa. 42:1. Judgement in the *'day of Christ'* will put right what's wrong with **mankind**, with the **world** and with the **earth** itself.

As to **mankind** our biggest problem has long been blindness and deafness toward God and His word. But in the *'day of Christ'* every Gentile on earth will be given **light to see** (see Isa. 49:6 above).

Silencing the world's chatter

But how will this be achieved, you ask? The answer is that in the *'day of Christ'*, the Lord will shut down the world's noisy, blatant chatter (Ps. 12:3) so that nothing is seen but His glory and nothing is heard but his word. That word on the *'breath of his lips'* (Isa. 11:4) will destroy the wicked but bring great blessings to the poor, to the oppressed, and to those who hear and believe his word. Consider these verses:

> Ps. 12:3 - *The Lord shall cut off all flattering lips, and the tongue that speaketh proud things: who have said, with our tongue will we prevail; our lips are our own: who is lord over us?*

> Isa. 29:18 - *And in that day shall the **deaf** hear **the words of the book** and the **eyes of the blind shall see** out of obscurity and darkness.*

> Isa. 40:5 - *And the **glory** of the Lord shall be revealed and **all flesh shall see it together**: for the mouth of the Lord hath spoken it.*

> Num.14:21 - *But as truly as I live **all the earth** shall be **filled** with the **glory of the Lord**.*

> Hab.2:14 - *For the **earth** shall be filled with the **knowledge** of the **glory** of the Lord as the waters cover the sea.*

Sing hallelujah, won't you? Because all these verses are promises, not just to Israel, but to *'all flesh'* and *'all the earth'*. The blessings of the Lord in his pre-millennial reign during the *'day of Christ'* will abound to all peoples with Gentiles receiving first priority, since the first order of business will be to *'bring forth judgement to the Gentiles'* (Isa. 42:1).

What a huge difference it will make when the glory of the Lord is revealed and **all flesh** shall see it together. Darkness will flee away and the curse of unbelief will be banished. It will be unthinkable to do anything else but worship and obey the Lord.

Importantly, His salvation will be sent '*unto the ends of the earth*'. Geographically New Zealand might be considered an end of the earth - it's just about as far as you can get away from Jerusalem without turning back - but that is not what scripture means.

In Bible truth '*the ends of the earth*' are people, people farthest out from God, those most in need of salvation. They are the desperate, poor, oppressed and hungry for God, though they may not know it. It is they who will hear, see and rejoice in the Lord's salvation in the '*day of Christ*'.

Think of the masses held in cruel darkness in the '*ends of the earth*' where Islam, communism, greedy capitalism, Buddhism, Hinduism, gross materialism, poverty, slavery, deviltry, and other '*works of darkness*' hold sway. These are the captives who need to be set free, the blind who need to see the Lord's glory shining down from heaven. And they will see and will be set free '*in that day*'.

I truly believe that the billions in the world now blinded by Satan to the wonders of God's grace in our present dispensation would have their eyes opened to see the glory of the Lord and hear His voice were they to live in the '*day of Christ.*' I also believe the time for that day is very near and some alive now may well live on to see the Lord's **appearing** (1 Tim. 6:14; 2 Tim. 4:1,8; Titus 2:13).

For it is at his **appearing** (Greek; *epiphaneia*, meaning a blazing forth) that the Lord will powerfully broadcast his glory on earth and at the same time step in to take over government of the world.

What's more, the Lord's promise to put things right reaches beyond people to all other creatures. '*All flesh*' will see the glory of the

Lord and that includes the restoration of the animal kingdom and all that live and move.

All people will be blessed

Yes, under the Lord's future rule from heaven all people on earth will be blessed and then from them the King will then begin his work of calling out his people Israel and restoring them to their land. Those who respond will comprise the true Israel of biblical prophecy. Again, it should be noted that the present 'State of Israel' is man's contrivance, not God's work. It isn't to be found in the Bible and, most of its people don't believe God's word and still reject their true Messiah, Jesus.

As to the **world**, there will be huge change for the better. Eph. 2:2 informs us that right now, the world's course runs '*according to the prince of the power of the air, the spirit that now worketh in the children of disobedience'.* In the bright new '*day of Christ'* to come it will be run by '*the great God and our Saviour Jesus Christ'* (Titus 2.13) from heaven. This is the same Lord who in Isa. 66:1 says:

The heaven is my throne and the earth is my footstool…

As to the **earth**, in our time its original beauty has been all but destroyed by man's sin, greed, destruction and exploitation. Only in the last rain forests, in special reserves, on rocky islands and in the icy wastes of Antarctica do the rarest animals and birds survive. Defiance of God and wicked idolatry have turned most of Africa into desert and evil has wrought famines, earthquakes, poverty, tempests and tsunamis around the globe. But the *'day of Christ'* will change all that. Our great King will restore nature to its original pre-flood glory.

> Isa. 35:1-2 - *… the desert shall rejoice and blossom as the rose. It shall blossom abundantly and rejoice even with joy*

> and singing ... they shall see the glory of the Lord and the excellency of our God.

> Isa. 11:6-9 - *The wolf will also dwell with the lamb, and the leopard shall lie down with the kid; and the calf and the young lion and the fatling together: and a little child shall lead them.*

> *And the cow and the bear shall feed; their young ones shall lie down together: and the lion shall eat straw like the ox. And the sucking child shall play on the hole of the asp, and the weaned child shall put his hand on the cockatrice.*

> *They shall not hurt nor destroy in all my holy mountain: for the earth shall be full of the knowledge of the glory of the Lord as the waters cover the sea.*

All this and more will be accomplished in the '*day of Christ*' which begins with the Lord's appearing from heaven in all His glory so that He can be seen by all on earth as God the Father sees Him. Thus, in his letter to Titus the Apostle Paul says the very reason that '*the grace of God which bringeth salvation hath appeared unto all men*' in our day is so that:

> *... denying ungodliness and worldly lusts we should live soberly, righteously and godly in this present world,* **looking** *for that blessed hope and the* **appearing** *of our great God and Saviour Jesus Christ.* (Titus 2:12-13)

I believe that three things will move the Lord to suddenly bring in his bright new day. The plight of the poor and oppressed is one (Ps. 12:5) – '*For the oppression of the poor, for the sighing of the needy, now will I arise, saith the Lord*'. The ruin of His once beautiful creation is another.

But the greatest motivation for Him will surely be when his people believe his word and understand the huge blessings the '*day of*

Christ' promises. Then they will cry out to the Lord to bring in *'his day'* (John. 8:56). Then they will pray and be *'looking'* daily for Him to do so (Titus 2:13). Here *'looking for'* means much more than merely keeping a 'look out'. It means eagerly anticipating this stupendous event; indeed, acting in faith as though it is already here.

As I first wrote this a long drought was ending in New Zealand's North Island. For months we had been looking daily for clouds and rain as the sun baked both garden and field brown. Then the rain finally came and *'renewest the face of the earth'* (Ps. 104:30).

Just as the parched earth cries out for the rain, so we must be **looking** for His **appearing**. One reason to do so is that judgement in the *'day of Christ'* will be a joyful thing. Our Lord Jesus Christ is a God of equity and justice. This is why Ps. 98:4-9 summons all the earth to:

> *Make a joyful noise before the Lord the King ... for He cometh to judge the earth; with righteousness shall He judge the world and the people with equity".*

Saints will be revealed in glory

In His judgment our Lord will destroy the wicked and ensure that the poor and the humble get what is right and fair, arguably for the first time in history. It will be as He promised in Matt. 5:5- *'Blessed are the meek, for they shall inherit the earth'.* They will inherit the earth because the Lord will first remove from power those who would keep it from them. Thus in Isa. 11:4 we are told:

> *But with righteousness shall He judge the poor, and reprove with equity for the meek of the earth: and He shall smite the earth with the rod of his mouth and with the breath of his lips shall He slay the wicked.*

If like me, you're sick of the lies, repression, godlessness and cruelty of this world and your trust is in the Saviour the Lord Jesus Christ, then it's wonderful to know those following Paul and his revelatory teaching will be revealed in glory to have a part in governing it. (see Col. 3:3-4). Right now the going is tough but as 2 Tim. 2:12 says:

> *If we suffer, we shall also reign with Him: if we deny Him, He will also deny us.*

Part Two

> Isaiah 24:21-22 - *And it shall come to pass* **in that day** *that the Lord shall punish the host of high ones that are on high and the kings of the earth upon the earth. And they shall be gathered together as prisoners are gathered together in the pit and shall be shut up in the prison, and after many days shall they be visited.*

Why is it that evil spiritual powers from on high can bedevil this world with apparent immunity? Fact is *'the rulers of the darkness of this world'* (Eph. 6:12) have been deceiving and destroying mankind for thousands of years. Yet it seems that to date they go unpunished by God.

Granted, the *'sons of God'* that *'kept not their own estate but left their habitation'* (Jude 6) to go in unto women (Gen. 6:2) are held in chains in darkness, reserved unto the day of judgement. But the Lord has not so punished those rebellious angels who stopped short of this crime but committed many others against humanity. He has not taken vengeance upon them. Indeed, for almost all of human history the *'principalities and powers'* seem to have gotten away with mismanaging the nations and committing wicked spiritual misdeeds.

Seduced by doctrines of devils

In our day, far from tolerating these dark rulers, we are called to *'wrestle against'* the authors of *'spiritual wickedness in high places'* (Eph. 6:12). But so successful are these *'seducing spirits'* (1 Tim. 4:1), that as a result of their efforts almost the whole world is immune to the gospel. Furthermore, in these *'latter times'* there is widespread departure from the faith within the ranks of professing Christendom.

Indeed, billions have been seduced by *'doctrines of devils'* into rejecting the very truth that could save them. Having abandoned biblical doctrine, they can be found *'speaking lies in hypocrisy, their conscience seared with a hot iron'* (1 Tim. 4:2). Observing this we know we are in the last days of the grace dispensation.

What's more, the devil continues the terrible work he began by corrupting mankind in the Garden of Eden nearly 6,000 years ago. And, helped by a host of renegade evil angels, he still corrupts them today. Make no mistake, *'this present evil world'* (Gal. 1:4) is ruled by Satan through his dark cohorts. Believers must take the whole armour of God to *'withstand in the evil day'* (Eph. 6:13), because Satan's forces still hold sway and seemingly still go unpunished at present.

But all this is about to change. Very soon these dark satanic rulers will get their comeuppance. This will happen in the *'day of Christ'*, that great event marked as 'next' on God's calendar. The good news today is that by faith believers can lay hold of and personally experience in advance the scriptural truth of this imminent occurrence. Col. 1:13, for example, tells those who will believe it that **already**, *'The Father hath delivered us from the power of darkness and translated us into the kingdom of his dear Son'.*

When we think of all the misery and murder, the blindness of heart and rejection of God that the devil's angels have caused throughout history we should be very angry with them. They have deceived the whole world and brought unspeakable evil and suffering on every generation of mankind.

They control the governments, banks, armies and thinking of this world and condemn many of its inhabitants to poverty. In the name of religion, they have murdered and tortured untold millions down the ages. Through the teaching of evolution, they have blindsided the whole world into ignorance of the Creator and his blessings.

Thank God that tomorrow in the *'day of Christ'* due sentence will be pronounced and executed against the evil powers that are on high. Their punishment in and of itself will be one of the greatest blessings ever extended to Gentiles, indeed to the whole world, *'in that day'*.

By the way, to avoid confusion it is important to understand that the words *'in that day'* comprise a code for the *'day of Christ'* when found in the psalms and prophetic scriptures. Occasionally, however, the phrase is used of the Lord's future 1,000-year reign on earth and where that is so usually the words *'day of the Lord'* will be found in the context.

Bear in mind that the *'day of the Lord'* is when the Lord personally visits the earth and its rebellious people with fiery judgement and war (Joel 2:3-11 and 2 Thess. 1:7-8). As such it sharply contrasts with and follows the *'day of Christ'* in which mankind will be blessed with seeing and hearing the Lord revealed in His kingdom glory.

Punishing the high ones on high

So, while there will be judgement in the *'day of Christ'* there will also be much blessing. The earth, for example, will be restored to its pre-flood beauty and plenty and be filled with the glory of the Lord.

Another important difference between these two great 'days' of God - each likely lasting for around 1,000 years (2 Pet. 3:8) - is that while rebellious man is destroyed in the *'day of the Lord'* it is rather the wicked spirits who are punished in the *'day of Christ'*.

Perhaps we can now see that without punishing Satan and his evil hordes no such blessing could be brought forward to all men. Consequently, I believe it is at the Lord's actual *'appearing'* (Titus 2:13) that the process of punishing the high ones on high will begin.

Traditional interpretations of Isa. 24:21 connect this 'punishment' with Satan being locked up (Rev. 20:1-7) during the Lord's future 1,000-year reign or associate it with the battle of Armageddon. But this connection cannot be for Isa. 24:23 specifically refers to the Lord of Hosts (who is Jehovah or Yahweh, i.e., Jesus Christ) reigning *'gloriously'*, that is, in glory, and there is no mention of Him doing so in either Rev. 16 or Rev. 20. Furthermore, the Lord's glorious rule must be in heaven and not on earth since it will confound the moon and make the sun ashamed (Isa. 24:23).

It is thought by some that the words *'...the Lord of Hosts shall reign in mount Zion and in Jerusalem'* refer to the Lord's 'coming' (Greek: *parousia*), i.e., his return to reign at his personal, physical return to earth. But actually, it is his rule from heaven that is in view here. *'Mount Zion and Jerusalem'* are employed to figuratively depict the effect of his heavenly kingdom as He rules over the earth in the *'day of Christ'*.

In Isa. 66:1 the Lord Himself states of this period: *'The heaven is my throne and the earth is my footstool'*, and that should settle that matter. In sharp contrast in the *'day of the Lord'* we are even told where the Lord's feet will physically stand on a mountain outside Jerusalem at His coming to earth (see Zech. 14: 1, 3 and 4 and Acts 1:11). And then indeed He will physically and personally reign from the Holy City.

One can only try to imagine the effect the Lord's **appearing** in heaven in his fullest power and glory will have on principalities and powers that now rule over nations and keep mankind in darkness. Suddenly, after some 6,000 years, their reign is over, their authority gone. For them this will be severe punishment. As Heb. 2:5 teaches, *'For unto the angels hath He not put in subjection the world to come, whereof we speak'*. And the *'world to come'* is of course the *'day of Christ'* Paul wrote of in 1 Cor. 1:7, Phil. 2:16 and elsewhere.

This punishment of angels will be made worse for them by the fact that their positions of power will be taken over by what to them are the lowest and most despised of creatures - redeemed men and women, saints who have been promised that if they suffer and die with Christ, they will also reign with Him in the day of Christ (2 Tim. 2:11-12).

Unbearable ignominy

This, I believe, is what is meant by the Lord punishing the host of the high ones that are on high. Their power will be stripped from them, their place in heaven will be forfeit and they will be herded into a prison from which there is no escape.

For such lofty spiritual beings, the shame and ignominy will be unbearable. The sheer light of the Lord's glory will drive them into a dark place. In fact, so bright is the Lord's glory that, though sinless themselves, even the moon and sun blush as they are put in the shade by His **appearing** (Isa. 24:23).

As to the effect down 'here below', it is no wonder Isa. 24:1 says the Lord *'...maketh the earth empty, maketh it waste and turneth it upside down'*. For as the Lord's shining forth in heaven banishes dark spiritual rulers from their thrones on high, so it also pricks like a balloon the power they exercise on earth through their appointed evil human rulers. Bear in mind that '*mountains*' in scripture depict earthly kingdoms and '*valleys*' those that are oppressed by them.

To '*prepare the way of the Lord ... every mountain shall be brought low and every valley shall be filled*', scripture says. This 'governmental' road-making will happen on an enormous, epoch-changing scale in the '*day of Christ*'. The Lord will harshly punish earthly rulers who derive their power from the evil principalities on high.

While the key verse in this study, Isa. 24:21-22, clearly marks out '*the host of the high ones that are on high*' and their puppet rulers, '*the kings of the earth upon the earth*', for drastic punishment, it should not be thought that the devil escapes unscathed:

> Isa. 27: 1 - **In that day** *the Lord with His sore and great and strong sword shall punish leviathan the piercing serpent, even leviathan that crooked serpent; and He shall slay the dragon that is in the sea.*

My understanding of this verse is that it speaks of the devil, the serpent that deceived the first man and woman in the Garden of Eden. However, the serpent is seen here as leviathan, '*the dragon that is in the sea*'. The picture is that of the serpent as it slithers among the seething mass of humanity (the '*sea*'), deceiving here, corrupting there and blockading people from the truth and work of God.

Isaiah's words bring to mind Israel's ancient enemies, Assyria, Babylon and Egypt, depicted by the serpent resident in their respective rivers, the Tigris, Euphrates and the Nile. Thus, there is the '*piercing serpent*' of Assyria, the '*crooked serpent*' of the winding Euphrates of Babylon and the '*dragon that is in the sea*', the crocodile of the Nile.

But the wider picture is that of the serpent's work in the world as a whole. The Apostle Paul in Eph. 2:2 describes him as '*the prince of the power of the air, the spirit that now worketh in the children of disobedience'.*

The serpent 'cut to the quick'

In the *'day of Christ'* the serpent's power and work will be cut short by the sword of God. His lies will be exposed as God's truth blazes forth to all mankind; his punishment will be to lose power over the kingdoms of this world, as both he and they are eclipsed by the Lord's *'appearing and his kingdom'* (2 Tim. 4:1*)*. He will be so cut to the quick he will have no influence on earth for hundreds of years.

For us it is hard to see the full power and the irresistible effect the Lord will have when He fully shows forth his glory power and truth in the *'day of Christ'* but the following verses give some insight into how our Lord will bless Gentiles at this time:

> Numbers 14:21 - *But as truly as I live, all the earth shall be filled with the glory of the Lord.*
>
> Isaiah 11:9 - *They shall not hurt nor destroy in all my holy mountain: for the earth shall be full of the knowledge of the Lord, as the waters cover the sea.*

Part Three

> Jn. 12:31,32 - *Now is the judgement of this world; now shall the prince of this world be cast out. And I, if I be* **lifted up from the earth**, *will draw all men unto Me.*
>
> Isa. 6:1 - *In the year that king Uzziah died I saw also the Lord sitting upon a throne, high and* **lifted up**, *and his train filled the temple.*
>
> 1 Tim. 6:14-15 - *…until the* **appearing** *of our Lord Jesus Christ, which in His times He* **shall shew** *who is the*

> *Blessed and Only Potentate, the King of kings and Lord of lords.*
>
> Isa. 40:5 - *And the **glory** of the Lord shall be **revealed** and all flesh shall see it, for the mouth of the Lord hath spoken it.*

Soon the Lord will *'draw all men'* unto Himself. *'All men'*, of course, means Gentiles, all people in fact, including Jewish people.

Some quibble with the *'all'* in Jn. 12:32 and assert that since in their belief God only saves those whom He chooses, *'all'* here does not mean all. But actually, it does. Their error stems from a refusal to recognise that Jn. 12:32 is prophetic and does not operate in our time but will most definitely take place in the time to come. But we, as serious Bible students, believe the Lord said what He meant and meant what He said. Therefore, if Christ said that if He is lifted up, He will draw **all** men unto Him, then that is what He will do. That is what will happen. The important question is, when?

Jn. 12:33 tells us that the Lord's saying, *'If I be lifted up from the earth, I will draw all men unto Me',* signified what death He should die. And the unbelieving Jews He was addressing took it to mean just that. They said (vs. 34): *'We have heard that Christ* (i.e., the Messiah) *liveth for ever and how sayest Thou, the Son of Man must be lifted up? Who is this Son of man?'* Clearly, they understood that He meant He would be *'lifted up'* by being crucified and they could not conceive of the Messiah dying at all. Therefore, they concluded, Jesus could not be the Messiah and they simply ignored his words about drawing all men unto Him.

When are all men drawn to Christ?

But does our Lord's death on the cross exhaust the meaning of *'I, if I be lifted up'?* No, it does not. This is made clear if we consider his plain statement that *'I will draw all men unto Me'.*

When were all men drawn unto Christ? Was it at the cross? No. There the people and the rulers derided Him, saying He saved others, let Him save Himself, and the soldiers also mocked Him (Luke 23:35-36). Perhaps the only ones truly changed in their heart at that time by His death were the thief on the cross and the Roman centurion who said *'…surely this was the Son of God'.*

Many would spiritualise the phrase *'I will draw all men unto Me',* and say that Christ even now is drawing all men unto Him by His cross. But this cannot be true because in every generation since that of his death for our sin, the majority of mankind has shunned the loving Saviour and His offer of salvation.

So, were *'all men'* drawn at his resurrection? No, because actually no one saw Him rise. Were they then drawn when He **appeared** after His resurrection? No, because Paul in 1 Cor. 15:5-8 states that the Lord was seen of the apostles, of Paul himself and *'of above five hundred brethren at once'.* Clearly, that does not amount to *'all men'.*

Nor was there mass conversion of people at his ascension. Actually, only his apostles saw Him ascend to heaven (Acts 1:2-10). True, a little later the Lord appeared on earth to call Paul as the Apostle to the Gentiles (Acts chapters 9, 22 and 26), but all men were not drawn at this time, nor have they been since.

Fact is, that never once in all human history to date has the Lord drawn all men unto Himself. Of course, you could argue, and many would, that the Lord indeed draws all men to Himself but most won't respond. But Jesus did not say He would draw all men only to see the majority refuse. He said: *'I will draw all men unto Me'*. And indeed, He will.

To 'draw' means to exert force, to pull an object or person towards a stated destination, in this case, *'all men unto Me'*. In John 21:6, 11 it is used of drawing a net full of fishes. In John 6:44 Jesus explains how salvation was effected at that time: *'No man can come unto Me, except the Father which hath sent Me **draw** him…'* Acts 16:19 speaks of Paul and Silas being forcibly seized, that is 'drawn', and taken before magistrates. However, the force our Lord will exert in drawing all men is His grace, kindness and overwhelming love. This is prophetically spoken of as a future event for Israel in Jer. 31:3:

> *Yea, I have loved thee with an everlasting love: therefore with loving kindness have I drawn thee.*

Consider the words, *'And I, if I be lifted up'*. The Greek word for *'lifted up'* is *hupsoo* which, like its Hebrew equivalent in the Old Testament, is mostly translated as '*exalted*'. So, does this mean that our Lord will draw all men unto Him when He is exalted? Indeed, it does. (The serious Bible student will find that *hupsoo* appears as '*exalted*' in Acts 2:33, 5:31, Matt. 23:12, 12; 11:23 and Luke 1:52. It appears as '*lifted up'* in John 3:14, 12:31-32, 8:28 and James 4:10).

Now in John 3:14 the Lord stated that *'…as Moses **lifted up** the serpent in the wilderness, even so must the Son of Man be **lifted up** that whosoever believeth on Him should not perish but have eternal life'*. Here '**lifted up**' certainly refers to His death on the cross and its saving power, particularly for the nation Israel. But, please note, very significantly the Lord does not talk about his drawing all men unto Him in this passage. Rather He says:

> *That **whosoever** believeth in Him should not perish but have eternal life.*

Now it is no coincidence, but a divine arrangement by the Holy Spirit, that those same English words **'lifted up'**, are also used in Isa. 6:1 where the great Hebrew prophet tells of seeing the Lord *'... sitting upon a throne,* **high and lifted up***'.* And here the words do speak of an event which will draw all men unto Him.

Here the Lord is not seen on the cross but on a throne and, since the throne is *'high',* it must be in heaven. Therefore, it must refer to the Lord's yet to be revealed *'heavenly kingdom'* (2 Tim. 4:18). Furthermore, this throne is Christ's own throne, not his Father's throne, signifying that now Christ fully rules as God in his own right.

This kingdom, in which Christ rules from heaven, precedes and is very different to that of the *'day of the Lord'* in which Christ will rule '*with a rod of iron'* personally from His physical throne in Jerusalem.

In fact, this yet to be but soon new eon which Jesus Christ said is '*My day'* (John 8:56), is the glorious age in which the Lord will show that indeed He is *'the blessed and only potentate'* (1 Tim. 6:15). He will do this *'...at his* **appearing** *and his* **kingdom***'* (2 Tim. 4:1).

By the way, did you know in the liturgical church calendars no single day is celebrated as 'Christ's Day'? Yes, there is Christmas Day, Easter and Whitsunday but no day is set aside exclusively for the Lord Jesus Christ Himself as He is now. What a telling omission! Yet the *'day of Christ'* will be a centuries-long eon when our Lord will display Himself fully as the rightful ruler of heaven and earth.

Amazingly, the glory of this soon to be event was what Isaiah foresaw (Isa. 6:1) some 2,700 years ago.

Let's see what he saw. The words, *'His train filled the temple',* speak of the Lord as King having conquered all his enemies. It was an ancient eastern custom for conquerors to cut off not only the heads of kings they defeated but also the *'train'* of their ceremonial robes. The snipped off *'train'* of cloth would then be sewn on to the conqueror's own mantle to add to its length. In Isaiah's vision of Christ ruling in glory from heaven, the Lord is seen as having conquered, or 'drawn' if you will, so many enemies at his **appearing** (Titus 2:13) and enthronement that his long flowing train fills the temple.

And truly here He is seen drawing all men unto Him, his greatest conquest of all. His glory shines forth from heaven and is irresistibly revealed to all men (Isa. 40:5):

> *And the **glory** of the Lord shall be **revealed** and all flesh shall see it, for the mouth of the Lord hath spoken it.*

In this there is prophesied the fulfilment of God's wonderful promise in Phil. 2:8-10:

> *… He humbled Himself and became obedient unto death, even the death of the cross. Wherefore also God hath **highly exalted** Him and given Him a name which is above every other name. That at the name of Jesus every knee should bow and every tongue confess that Jesus Christ is Lord to the glory of God the Father.*

The words *'highly exalted'* in this passage translate the Greek word *huperupsoo*, which means to exalt above any other. This is what our Lord meant when He said *'I, if I be lifted up, will draw all men unto Me'*. He would draw all men unto Him when He was lifted above all principality and power, above every name on earth and in heaven, both now and in the age to come.

An irresistible sight

Phil. 2:9 makes plain that Christ Jesus has already been highly exalted by the Father. And believers taught by grace know they have been exalted with Him; that is, they have been *'made to sit together in heavenly places in Christ'* (Eph. 2:6). But as of now this truth is hid from the world. *'Our life is hid with Christ in God'* and will only appear when we appear with Him in glory (Col. 3:3-4).

So, we see that *'all men'* will only know of Christ's exaltation, and that of the believers chosen to rule and reign with Him, at *'his appearing and kingdom'* (2 Tim. 4:1). This is when his divine majesty will be revealed; His glory will shine forth so powerfully not a person will be able to turn their eyes from the sight, nor stop their ears to its message. Then truly *'...every knee will bow and every tongue confess that Jesus Christ is Lord to the glory of God the Father'* (Phil. 3: 9-11).

But, I hear someone ask, how is this Pauline prediction linked to Isaiah's prophecies of the glorious kingdom to come? The short answer is: because it is based upon them. True, the dispensation of grace and the mystery of our being made one with Christ were *'hid in God'* and unprophesied in Isaiah's time, but the truth of the *'day of Christ'* and his ruling from glory was not. Actually, the theme of the Lord's kingdom runs throughout the Bible. In Acts 3:21 it is described as the:

> *Times of restitution of all things which God hath spoken by the mouth of all His holy prophets since the word began.*

Thus, if we turn to Isa. 45:22-23 we find God vowing that all men will be drawn and in doing so using the very words quoted by the Apostle Paul in Phil. 2:10-11:

> *Look unto Me and be ye saved, all the ends of the earth: for I am God and there is none else. I have sworn by Myself, the word is gone out of my mouth in righteousness, and shall not return. That unto Me* **every knee shall bow, every tongue shall swear.**

And in Isa. 40:5 we are told that the glory of the Lord shall be revealed and '*all flesh shall see it*'. This truth is echoed in Isa. 6:3 in the seraph's prophetic cry that '*the whole earth is full of His glory*'. Clearly then, only when the Lord is fully revealed in all His kingdom glory and that glory shines out for all on earth will all men be drawn unto Him. And, thank God, it is now the very next thing on his agenda.

Isa. 6:1 records a unique event. Isaiah becomes the first and only man to date to see the Lord (the Jehovah, or Yahweh, of the Old Testament who is the Christ Jesus of the New) sitting upon the (to us) future throne of His glory. Isaiah was divinely transported far into the future to see Him so **appear** in glory. For even now, in this current dispensation of the grace of God (Eph. 3:3), the Lord has yet to be enthroned in all his glory.

Consider these facts. Jesus at His trial told the high priest: '*Hereafter shall* **ye** (meaning Israel as a nation) *see the Son of man sitting at the* **right hand** *of power…*' (Matt. 26:64). The Apostle Peter said that God had raised up Jesus, to '*…sit Thou on my* **right hand** *until I make thy enemies thy footstool*' (Acts 2:34). The martyr Stephen saw '*…Jesus standing at the* **right hand** *of God*'(Acts 7:56). The Apostle Paul in Rom. 8:34, Eph. 1:20, Col. 3:1 confirms that as of now '*Christ* (still) *sitteth on the* **right hand** *of God …in the heavenly places*'.

How sin will be purged

But Isaiah saw the Lord '*sitting upon a throne* **high and lifted up**', not at the right hand of a throne. He saw the Lord, not sat at the right hand of the Father, but sat upon His own throne in glory in the heavenlies. What's more '*his train filled the temple*' and when a seraph cried, '*Holy, holy, holy is the Lord of hosts, the whole earth is full of his glory*', '*the house was filled with smoke*'. Now the latter phrase means that Isaiah saw the incense of his presence, that is his glory, filling the earth just as the Lord had vowed it would in Num. 14:21:

> *But as truly as I live all the earth shall be filled with the glory of the Lord.*

What's more, in this vision Isaiah saw sin being purged. Just as the Prophet Isaiah's '*unclean lips*' were cleansed in Isa. 6:5-7 so will the unclean lips of all those who confess the Lord's name be cleansed in his day. The purging comes from a coal taken off the altar of incense, which in the day of Christ will be the glory of His presence made manifest throughout earth and, indeed, unto all men.

Thus, the picture we should see in Isa. 6 is that of our Lord Jesus Christ being enthroned as *Jehovah Sabaioth* (the Lord of all the hosts of heaven and earth) and filling the earth with his glory. Isaiah saw the Lord of Hosts sat upon his own throne. He saw Jehovah (who is Jesus) keeping covenant with his creation and filling the earth with his glory.

The seraphim (verse 2) are 'burning ones' and cry *'holy, holy, holy is the Lord of hosts'*. The door posts move at their cry and the house is filled with smoke or cloud.

This teaches us that the Lord is not pictured here as the Shekinah presence between two cherubim on the mercy seat of the Ark of the Covenant but in glory upon his own throne and attended by seraphim, which are winged serpent-like creatures. As ones that burn, they evidently tend the altar of incense from which one of them takes a live coal with tongs and touches Isaiah's lips with it.

This is suggestive of the effect the revelation of the Lord's glory will have upon all men. They will be purged of speaking and believing the devil's lies about God. They will be drawn irresistibly to the brightness of His glory. In this way they will be convinced of the truth of the gospel and saved.

As Isa. 49:6 specifically states:

> *I will give thee also for a light to the Gentiles, that Thou mayest be my salvation unto the end of the earth.*

Even so Lord, we look for your light to shine forth in our time.

Chapter Fourteen - THE APPOINTED DAY OF JUDGEMENT

> Acts 17: 29-31 - *Forasmuch then as we are the offspring of God, we ought not to think that the Godhead is like unto gold, or silver, or stone, graven by art and man's device. And the times of this ignorance God winked at, but now commandeth all men everywhere to repent: Because* **He hath appointed a day, in the which he will judge the world in righteousness** *by that Man who he hath ordained: whereof He hath given assurance unto all men, in that He hath raised Him from the dead.*

> John 12:47 - *… I came not to judge the world, but to save the world.*

> Acts 10:42 - *And He (Jesus) commanded us to preach unto the people and to testify that it is He which was ordained of God to be the Judge of quick and dead.*

> Matthew 12 - 18 and 20: *Behold my Servant … I will put my Spirit upon Him and he shall shew judgement unto the Gentiles … till He send forth judgement unto victory.*

> 2 Tim: 4:1 - (Paul to Timothy) *I charge thee therefore before God, even the Lord Jesus Christ who shall judge the quick and the dead at his appearing and his kingdom.*

If there's a message everyone needs to hear and heed today it is that God has appointed a **set day** to judge the world in righteousness. Why? Because this is the best news we as people could ever hear. You see, for thousands of years men have striven to bring about a better world, yet today society is more evil than when they began. It seems we humans are incredibly slow to learn that only Almighty God can reshape the world from the mess it is now into the paradise He intends it to be.

Given that mankind suffers incurable disease, death, poverty, and other evils, there should be rejoicing on every hand that God has predetermined a set time to intervene in human affairs to set right that which is wrong. Yet there isn't, because the proclamation of the 'appointed day' to change history for ever is studiously ignored by the world.

Nevertheless, God's word is true. The dawning of this great day will usher in a new world in which sickness, death, sin, war and even economic exploitation will be banished. For God Himself will rule the earth and all in it and only one belief system will be allowed – his. *'In that day'* all will know Him and submit to Him. This 'set day' is denoted seven times in Paul's epistles as the *'day of Christ'* and heralded by Old Testament prophets as the eon when *'…all the earth shall be filled with glory of the Lord'* (Num. 14:21).

For us who live in this *'present evil world'* (Gal. 1:4) it's high time to face facts. To recognise that for all our much-vaunted wisdom and technological advance life for most of earth's inhabitants is only getting worse. Cruelty, starvation, poverty, ecological disaster, murder, rape, slavery and war are escalating. Not to mention insecurity and fear. Man is not evolving into a better being; he is becoming more selfish and evil. The truth is that only God can halt humanity's slide to self-destruction; the divine good news announced in Athens by the Apostle Paul, and relayed to us through the Bible, is that He most definitely will.

God will intervene

What can make the world a better place except a powerful and unprecedented intervention by Almighty God who alone has power to change the heart of man and the world he lives in? Let us suppose that just such a huge change for the better really is coming. That there will indeed be an eon (a wonderful new age) when things will be put right, not made worse, for the earth and all who live on it. If that is so then all the conclusions of science, education, economics, politics, medicine and psychology, about both the present and the future, stand to be upset like the proverbial apple cart.

Now, it is highly significant that it is on Mar's Hill in Athens, the centre of world thinking in its day - and not Jerusalem or Rome - that God chose to proclaim this great news (Acts 16:31). He did so because the promise of this new day is to the world as a whole, to every nation, not just Israel. The timing was also critical. In 53 AD the Acropolis was a great seat of learning. It was home to the *Areopagus*, which debated and decided matters of belief, justice and government, not just for Athens but for the Greek world and beyond. Thus, the Areopagus was at once debating chamber, university, High Court and seat of Government all rolled into one. So deep was Greek thinking then that its philosophic theories still greatly influence us today.

And it was to this Areopagus on Mars' Hill in 53 AD that the Apostle Paul was summoned to answer for his preaching of *'strange gods'* (as the Athenians termed it) and for promulgating 'a new doctrine', that of Jesus and his resurrection (Acts 17:18). Such a trial was no light matter. On this very spot the Areopagus condemned the famed philosopher Socrates to death by suicide for 'impiety against the pantheon of Athens' and 'corrupting' Athenian youth by 'refusing to recognise the gods acknowledged by the state, and importing strange divinities of his own' – in a nut shell, exactly what Paul was accused of doing.

However, so stunning were the words that God spoke through Paul in answer to these charges that penalty was averted. In fact, the Lord used the occasion to put all men, both then and now, on notice that, in response to the world judging his emissary Paul, He has fixed a day in which He will judge the world (Acts 17:31). In particular the Lord commanded that idolatry – the concrete evidence of which was all around Paul as he spoke – should cease. Instead, men should urgently submit to Him as the only God in light of the soon coming 'judgement day'.

Sadly, most Athenians took little notice of these marching orders from on high. Neither did the wider world of Paul's day give them credence. Nor is the *'day of judgement'* a popular sermon subject in churches today. Ironically, this, in large part, is due to the still pervading influence in Christendom, even today, of some of the pagan beliefs Paul withstood on Mars' Hill in 53 AD.

To this day major Christian denominations hold to the Amillennial position, setting aside the truth of both the Lord's 1,000-year reign upon earth and the *'day of Christ'* (in which He will indeed judge the world) which precedes it. Instead, they try to make Acts 17-29-30 teach there will be one 'last judgement' at which Christ will consign resurrected people either to a hell of 'eternal torment' or to heaven.

However, Paul's Mars Hill pronouncement says nothing about any individual's eternal destiny or a 'last judgement' at all. What it does say is that God will **judge the world in righteousness**. That is He will put right what is wrong with, *'this present evil world'* (Gal. 1:4), the course of which is currently determined by the devil, *'the spirit that now worketh in the children of disobedience'* (Eph. 2:2).

Furthermore, God will radically correct the world as a system. His government and his justice will take over. It will be blessing and reward, rather than penalty. Furthermore, it will not be a judgement unto punishment, rather, it will be a setting right of all that is wrong. That is why it is described as a *'judgement in righteousness'*. Stripped of the myths religion has told about Him, our *'great God and Saviour Jesus Christ'* is a fair and equitable God.

As the Psalmist foretold: *'With righteousness shall He judge the world and the people with equity'* (Ps. 98:9). Today, in too many cases, neither governments, nor the police, nor courts can deliver true justice. But God can and will. Ps. 67:4 spells this out:

> *O let the nations be glad and sing for joy; for Thou shalt judge the people righteously and govern the nations upon earth.*

It may be asked: Does God have a right to judge the world? The answer has to be a resounding 'yes'. After all, He not only created the earth and every living form it contains, He also gave man the right to govern himself (Gen. 9:1-7). Sadly, in the outcome, mankind turned from God and gave the devil control of his social system and habitat. Now, after more than 4,000 years of watching man misgovern himself by heeding Satan rather than God, the Lord will render his verdict on our efforts and He will do so in a stunning display of his love, mercy and grace.

Hearts changed to love Him

Indeed, He will so fully reveal his glory that every person on earth will know Him, hear Him and be caused to believe Him. As said elsewhere in these studies, the word *'appearing'* (2 Tim. 4:1, Tit. 2:13) is far too weak to correctly translate *epiphanea*, which means the full unveiling or shining forth in glory of Jesus Christ as the God of all power and might, who has been given the right to rule the nations because of his death for our sin and subsequent resurrection (Rom. 1:4).

Thus, when Christ blazes forth his glory as the 'man made God' through his death and resurrection and asserts his right to rule all on earth, then the hearts of men and women will be changed to love Him. Millions worldwide will be instantly converted, for *'all will see Him,'* as the great God and Saviour He truly is. As Col. 3:4 declares: *'When Christ who is our life shall appear* (i.e., blaze forth), then *shall ye also appear with Him in glory'.*

In the *'day of Christ'*, the day of righteous judgement, the world will see a great light. Ps. 77:18 prophetically says that when God's thunder is heard in heaven '*his lightnings lightened* (or enlightened) *the world; the earth trembled and shook.'*

As Jesus Himself said (Luke 17:24): *'For as the lightning that lighteneth out of the one part under heaven shineth unto the other part under heaven, so shall the Son of Man be in his day'*. It should go without saying that the 'lightning' here is Christ enlightening the world; it is not just the lightning of a thunderstorm.

Chapter Fifteen -
IS IT HIS REVELATION OR HIS COMING?

In 1 Cor. 1:7 the Apostle Paul described the state of the Corinthians and other Acts period believers as *'waiting for the coming of our Lord Jesus Christ'*. However, a little research shows that actually it was the **revelation** (or revealing) of Christ they were waiting for, not his 'Second Coming'.

The confusion stems from the difficulty translators of the King James Bible had with end time events. Like many today they did not believe there would be a special *'day of Christ'* in which from heaven He would reveal Himself in a blaze of unparalleled glory. Rather, they tended to see the organised 'church' on earth as reigning in his stead. So, they simply translated the several different Greek words for the Lord's future dealings with men as *'coming'*.

But *'coming'* is a poor translation of *apokulapsis* which in 1 Cor. 1:7 means an **unveiling** of that which has been hidden, or a '**revelation**', as explained in the KJV margin note. Today, like the Corinthians we too await that revelation or unveiling of the full glory of our Lord. Are we not told in Col. 3:1-4 that while at present both our life and Christ Himself are *'hid in God'*, in a future day He will appear in glory?

In 1 Cor. 1:7 it is certainly not the very different Lord's return to earth in the *'day of the Lord'* (1 Thess. 5:2) that is in view. If it were then the Greek word *parousia*, which means the personal, physical presence of a person to perform an official duty, would have been used. In 1 Thess. 4:15-16, for example, *'coming'* is used to translate *parousia* and does indeed indicate the personal, physical return of the Lord to earth. No, it is the *'day of Christ'*, the day of his *'appearing'* (Greek: *epiphaneia*) (Titus 2:13, 2 Tim. 4:1) that is referred to in 1 Cor. 1:7.

And *'coming'* doesn't even begin to describe what the Lord will do either in the *'day of Christ'* or in the subsequent *'day of the Lord'*.

Consider an example. When the Queen of Britain pays a state visit to New Zealand it is not just a 'coming'. If it were, she would alight from the plane, be greeted by the Governor-General, the Prime Minister and an array of other dignitaries, inspect the guard of honour, then promptly re-board the plane and fly out.

That would have been a 'coming'. In fact, the Queen always **stays** several days to carry out official functions. Similarly, when the Lord makes his *parousia* (his 'coming') in the *'day of the Lord'* (Zech. 14:1) He will touch down on the Mount of Olives (Zech. 14:4) and remain to rule for at least 1,000 years over the earth (Zech. 14:9, Rev. 11:15).

But long before then He will have already 'revealed' or 'unveiled' his person, his truth and his glory to the world (1 Cor. 1:7) in the *'day of Christ'*, though remaining in heaven while He does so (Acts 3:21). And this unveiling will continue for several centuries. As God said Himself in Num. 14:21: *'But as truly as I live, all the earth shall be filled with the glory of the Lord'*.

Since, according to 1 Cor. 1:8, it is in the *'day of our Lord Jesus Christ'* – not the *'day of the Lord'* - that the Corinthians are to be found *'blameless'*, it seems the *'coming'* - or when better translated, the *'revelation'* of Christ – continues throughout this, his new day.

And since the *'day of Christ'* is the same as the 'heavenly kingdom' or 'kingdom of heaven' that both Christ and the Apostle Paul spoke of, then qualifying to be resurrected into it is, and must be, the Christian's great and blessed hope (Titus 2:13).

While Christ remains in heaven during this period, He will rule the world by delegating authority to selected saints who have been resurrected to be on earth. These will be the ones who have been *'counted worthy'* to enter *'the world to come'*, just as Jesus said would be (Luke. 20:35).

Waiting for the Lord to rule in glory

Importantly, it is the Lord's exertion of his right to rule as Lord of all the earth that the Corinthians waited for. For it is his kingdom, his government that is his glory, a glory He will blaze forth at his 'appearing' (Titus 2:13, 2 Tim. 4:1 and Col. 3:1-4). The great good news the Apostle Paul has for us who believe these truths is that if we suffer with Him, we shall also reign with Him (2 Tim. 2:12); if we die with Him, we shall also live with Him (2 Tim. 2:11) and so *'appear with Him in glory'*.

But God does not want this wonderful truth of a far better world to come to be known only by the believers He has chosen to be part of his forthcoming Government. As previously outlined, in Acts 17:30-31 God speaks from Mars' Hill to all men, through Paul, the 'Apostle to the Gentiles', commanding *'all men everywhere to repent'* - that is, to have the 'after mind' of one who sets his or her future hope on the forthcoming kingdom of God and the role the Lord might assign to them in it.

To *'repent'* then means to fully submit to the Lord and to pray for, hope for, believe in and live for the day in which God will judge the world in righteousness, the *'day of Christ'*.

For God has promised that He will so judge the world *'by that Man* (i.e., Jesus Christ) *whom He hath ordained, whereof He hath given assurance in that He hath raised Him from the dead'* (Acts 17:31).

Chapter Sixteen -
THE GLORY TO FOLLOW

What is glory? The word runs like a river through all that scripture says about the 'day of Christ' and its synonyms, including 'the world to come', the 'day of rest', 'the times of the restoration of all things which God has spoken by the mouth of all his holy prophets since the world began' (Acts 3:21, NKJV). So much so the 'day of Christ' (1 Cor. 1:8) could well be called the 'day of his glory'.

Undoubtedly, God's glory is his grace and his salvation. 1 Pet. 1:10-11 makes this clear, speaking of the Old Testament prophets' inquiry as to what person or time *'...the Spirit of Christ who was in them did signify when it testified beforehand the sufferings of Christ and the glory that should follow.'*

Importantly, it is in his own glory that Christ will blaze forth at his **appearing** (Titus 2:13) which is the start of that glorious day when He will judge the quick and the dead and govern the world (2 Tim. 4:1). Indeed, it seems we are saved by the Lord's 'first' **appearing** in grace (Titus 2:11) mainly so that we can look for his 'second' **appearing** in glory (Titus 2:13).

You see, you can't see the *'great God and our Saviour Jesus Christ'* (Titus. 2:13) without also seeing the fullness of his glory. Indeed, He wants you to both see his glory and be glorified with Him in it (John 17:24, Col. 3:4).

Just as the glory of the risen exalted Christ will be put on show for all the world to see, so it will also be fully revealed in us who believe. Rom. 8:18 plainly states the *'...sufferings of this present time are not worthy to be compared to the glory that shall be revealed in* us'.* Indeed, our present *'light affliction which is but for a moment,* is *'working for us a far more and exceeding and eternal weight of glory'* (2 Cor. 4:17).

But what does God's glory really mean? Is it just his gracious act in forgiving and pardoning our sin through Christ's death on our behalf? No, it's more. For in Num. 14:20-21 the Lord relents and pardons Israel for her rebellion, then tells Moses:

> *I have pardoned according to your word. But as truly as I live all the earth shall be filled with the glory of the Lord.*

Mere pardon then is not God's idea of glory. But receiving we sinners in grace (Rom. 15:7), and restoring fallen mankind and the damaged earth to what both should be, is. And so also is resurrection. Indeed, just before raising Lazarus from the dead Jesus told Martha:

> *Did I not say to you that if you would believe you would see the glory of God?* (John 11:40).

And when that dead and buried man walked out from the tomb God's glory is what she saw. But even resurrection does not exhaust the meaning of the glory of God. There is far more, for God's glory outshines the sun. Perhaps the Bible's most superlative description of God's glory is found in Rev. 21:23 speaking of the New Jerusalem:

> *And the city had no need of the sun, neither of the moon to shine in it, for the glory of God did lighten it, and the Lamb is the light thereof.*

Saul was knocked to the ground by a glory brighter than the noon day sun in midsummer when the risen, fully empowered, fully glorified Lord appeared to him on the road to Damascus (Acts 26:13). In an instant he was changed from a hateful persecutor of believers to a loving servant and on the spot commissioned as the Apostle to the Gentiles.

Such is the effect when our Lord reveals Himself in glory to just one man. What will it be like when He displays his glory to the whole world? Because that is what He will do in the *'day of Christ'* – Isa. 40:5: *'The glory of the Lord shall be revealed and all flesh* (people) *shall see it together: for the mouth of the Lord hath spoken it'.*

Surely, His blazing forth of his glory to everyone on earth will have the same effect as it did on Saul. Mankind at large will repent and be saved there and then. This will be in his day, his day of glory. Didn't Jesus say that *'the world through Him should be saved'* (John 3:17 NASB)?

The glory of God within

Furthermore, if we are saved, then already we have the glory of God within. 2 Cor. 4:6 states: *'…for God has … shone in our hearts to give the light of the knowledge of the glory of God in the face of Jesus Christ.'*

Now, in one sense, God's glory has always shone, for, *'The heavens declare the glory of God'* (Ps. 19:1) and they have been doing so from creation until now. What's more, God is so glorious that when He unveils Himself the power is such men fall 'as dead' before Him.

The Apostle John, Daniel, Saul and others fell and the Prophet Isaiah cried, *'Woe is me for I am undone. Because I am a man of unclean lips; for my eyes have seen the King, the Lord of Hosts.'* (Isa. 6:1-5) Several of these were holy (that is, separated unto God) men, yet they were convicted to the core of their inherent sinfulness when the Lord shone in glory upon them. So, imagine, what the effect of the Lord Jesus Christ's displaying the full glory of his Person to the world will have on sinners in his day, the imminent *'day of Christ'* to come.

What's more, even now it is the Lord's glory, the power of his presence, albeit in veiled or diluted form, that keeps believers in this life and preserves them unto the next.

All said, it is no wonder one website writer tells us: '...glory is one of the buried treasures of lost humanity. It is an imprisoned splendour. The purpose and the power of God's glory delivers the keys for releasing his glorious life in a manifested demonstration of spiritual living and creative work'.

The bottom line is that without God's glory man is not what he should be. As Rom. 3:23 states: *'... all have sinned and fall short of the glory of God'.* And God is determined to put that right. You see, it is God's glory to restore human beings to the glory in God and of God they were created to have in the first place. Of course, that glory was lost through sin in the Garden of Eden. But Almighty God, the Lord Jesus Christ, was born as a man, overcame our temptations and poured out his blood in death to restore the glory we have lost.

For the record, the word 'glory' is used 148 times in Genesis, Exodus, Leviticus and Numbers, and from Deuteronomy to Malachi and on numerous occasions in the New Testament. It is the very essence of who God is and very soon He will shine it so powerfully the whole world will see and be changed in its light.

Believe it or not, it seems God finds his ultimate glory in you and me, those that believe on Jesus Christ as Saviour and Lord and give themselves to his purposes. Heb. 2:10 tells us that Jesus *'in bringing many sons to glory'* was Himself *'made perfect through sufferings'.*

In 1 Pet. 5:10, we learn that the *'God of all grace* (has) *called us unto his eternal glory'.* And in 1 Pet. 1:6-7 the Apostle declares that our faith, *'though tested by fire may be found to praise, honour and glory at the revelation* (i.e., **appearing**) *of Jesus Christ.'*

So, we are his glory and He, of course, is ours. What's more, God so delights in his glory He wants you and me to have it to the full and over-flowing. However, we will only receive the fullness of that in the glorious *'day of Christ'* which is even now at the very doors.

Prayer:

> *Dear Lord Jesus, like Moses, I too have found grace in your sight. You have called me by name and saved me by your precious blood. Now, just as Moses asked You to show him your glory (Exod. 33:13-18), so I also ask You to reveal your glory to Me. This, so that I can share the glory of who You are with others. I also ask, as Moses did, that You show me your way that I may know You more closely. And I ask that the very Presence of Yourself goes with me throughout my life's journey. Amen.*

Chapter Seventeen - WAS JESUS MADE SICK FOR US?

A discussion of whether total healing is included in our redemption or not.

The Prophet Isaiah and the Apostle Peter both say that we are healed by the whipping laid on the Messiah Jesus, the One crucified for our sins; (*'by whose stripes we are healed'*, see Isa. 53:5 and 1 Pet. 2:24).

However, many still question whether physical healing is really provided for us in the atonement Christ wrought on the cross. They have no doubt our Lord won forgiveness of sin and eternal life for us through his death, burial and resurrection. Indeed, no true Christian doubts that forgiveness, redemption and a restored relationship with God are instant upon belief (see John 5:24 and 1 John 3:14). As Paul told the Philippian jailer, 'Believe on the Lord Jesus and you will be saved, you and your family' (GNB). And in Rom. 10: 8-9 (GNB) he writes:

> *God's message is near you, on your lips and in your heart — that is, the message of faith that we preach. If you confess that Jesus is Lord and believe that God raised Him from death, you will be saved. For it is by our faith that we are put right with God; it is by our confession that we are saved. The scripture says, 'Whoever believes in Him will not be disappointed'. This includes everyone, because there is no difference between Jews and Gentiles; God is the same Lord of all and richly blesses all who call to Him.*

> *As the scripture says, 'Everyone who calls out to the Lord for help will be saved'.*

But is miraculous healing still available as one of 'rich blessings' promised upon belief in the Lord Jesus Christ or has it passed away? If it remains, is it available unconditionally in the same way forgiveness and reconciliation with God are given immediately upon confession of faith in the Lord? And if not (as they say in Parliament) why not? This chapter goes in search of the scriptural answers.

Importantly, it also notes that today both miracles and lasting healings seem in short supply, even in campaigns and crusades that proclaim present-day healing by Jesus. Indeed, a quick survey of the televised meetings of America's self-proclaimed healing ministries finds little evidence of clearly manifested miracles. True, some healings do occur; perhaps they just take longer.

However, the fact is that many with serious, chronic and even life-threatening conditions come away from such meetings no better than they came. And that is tragic, because today countless millions are seeking healing from Jesus; indeed, whole churches and other Christian organisations now see this as their main function.

It is also tragic that many, who trust in Christ as Saviour, hesitate to believe in Him as healer. Others know He can heal but doubt it is his will to do so. The real question, of course, is: do the Lord's sufferings provide physical healing as certainly as they do forgiveness of sin and salvation? Some answer that while healing of serious disease and physical ailments occasionally occurs, it is a sovereign and special act of God's grace; the exception rather than the rule.

Is God still in the healing business today?

Consequently, there is widespread doubt God is still seriously in the healing business today. Cessationists, for example, believe supernatural acts of God, along with spiritual gifts, stopped at the end of the Book of Acts coincident with the further revelation to Paul of God's grace and the mystery. However, while Paul said tongues would cease and prophecies and knowledge be done away with in 1 Cor. 13:8 he did not include miracles or healing in the disposal list.

What's more the context of the 'cessation' in 1 Cor. 13:8 is not that of a major dispensational change in God's dealings but that of a progressive maturing in the believer's walk. *'Childish things'* are *'put away'* in favour of abiding in *'faith hope and love'*. But miraculous healing is not mentioned as a blessing that will cease. It remains, even among the mature, for in Phil. 2: 26-28 Epaphroditus, a long-approved minister, was *'sick unto death'* but was miraculously healed when *'God had mercy on him'*.

Furthermore, if healing has stopped and miracles no longer available, as some dispensationalists hold, then the Lord Jesus would be found to be a liar, for He said, *'Most assuredly, I say unto you, he that believes in Me, the works that I do shall he do also, and greater than these shall he do, because I go unto the Father'* (John 14:12 ASV). In any age then believers can do the healing miracles Jesus did. He said so.

What then is the problem? Why is not physical healing as normative as forgiveness of sin and reconciliation with God in Christian experience? This chapter suggests that first, it is a failure to fully take God at his word, thus weakening faith, and second, a misunderstanding of the true nature of healing in the atonement in the first place. Without question it is an important issue, for many Christians today doubt whether God will heal when asked to do so, simply because so many prayers for healing seem to go unanswered.

So, we turn to the Bible, God's word, for the answers. To begin, it must be said that in both Old and New Testaments God strongly states, and demonstrates, that He is indeed the great Healer. *'I am the*

Lord who heals you,' He says in Exodus 15:26 (NKJV). Furthermore, He is the Lord *'...who **forgiveth** all thine iniquities; who **healeth** all the diseases; who **redeemeth** thy life from destruction; who crowneth thee with loving kindness and tender mercies'* (Ps.103: 3-4).

On earth Jesus spent much time healing the multitudes of sick, afflicted and demon-possessed who came to Him. Arguably, He expended more energy in doing this that He did in administering forgiveness of sins. And it wasn't only an odd person here or there who was restored to perfect health, as it seems to be today.

> *'He cast out the spirits with his word and healed **ALL** that were sick.'* (Matt. 8:16)

> Luke 6:19: *'...and the whole multitude sought to touch Him, for there went virtue of Him and healed them **ALL**.'*

Is the Lord still the same today?

Should healing happen now as it did then? In Mal. 3:6 we are told: *'For I AM the Lord; I change not'*. Heb. 13:8 insists: *'Jesus Christ is the same yesterday, today and for ever'* (NKJV). Both Isa. 53: 4 and 1 Pet. 2:24 insist that *'by his stripes we **ARE** healed'*. Not, we **WERE** healed. Not, we **WILL** be healed (maybe). But we **ARE** (already) healed because today Jesus Christ is still the Lord, *'who healeth all thy diseases'*. We should simply trust in it as an accomplished fact.

And if our diseases are being healed continuously as plain scripture asserts, then what we have in the atonement is ongoing good health, rather than a series of sickness attacks from which we have to be specially healed by God having mercy on us. In other words, if we fully accept that Jesus on the cross was made sin for us and also was made sick with all our diseases (so that we don't have to be) then we have good health as a gift from the Lord.

'Every whit whole' is how Jesus describes his healing ministry in John 7:23. The phrase translates the Greek word *holos* from which we get the English word 'holistic', a buzzword for medical treatment seeking to treat the whole person, physically mentally, spiritually and even socially. Jesus then, was, and still is, (since He doesn't change) a holistic healer. Example: in Acts 9:34 the Apostle Peter used his delegated authority from the Lord to tell the paralysed and bed-ridden Aeneas, *'Jesus Christ maketh thee whole'* - and Aeneas got up immediately.

And, if we are made *'every whit whole'* then there should be no incomplete or drawn-out healings, no lingering sicknesses or un-healed conditions. Rather we should be in prevailing good health. And, indeed, that is evidenced by some sincere Christians who do not attend healing meetings (because they are not sick) but nevertheless enjoy good health well into old age.

Should we get ill in the first place?

If you will accept it, as much as the Lord's death in taking our sin upon Him made us righteous in God's sight, thus making us 'holy', his being made sick for us on the cross makes us whole and healthy. Thus, if we fully believe and receive the atonement, we should not get seriously ill in the first place.

It's vital we understand by faith that we are *'made whole'*, because if Christ did not fully atone (i.e., make right) for all that is wrong with us through his holy life, death, resurrection and ascension then we cannot be fully saved and preserved in spirit, soul and body (1 Thess. 5:23), as the Apostle Paul said we will be.

The issue then is what we believe. To that end we now look at scriptures from various translations that strongly assert that not only was Jesus *'... made **sin** for us that we might become the righteousness* *of God in Him'* (2 Cor. 5:21 NKJV) but also that He Himself also bore our **sicknesses** both in his earthly ministry and on the tree.

Various Bible versions are considered because poor translation in the King James Bible and some others obscure the truth on this issue. For example, while the KJV talks in Isa. 53:4 of Christ bearing our **griefs**, the NASB (New American Standard Bible) unequivocally proclaims:

> *However, it was our **sicknesses** that He Himself bore, and our **pains** that He carried; yet we ourselves assumed that He had been afflicted, struck down by God, and humiliated.*

The NRSV (New Revised Standard Version) says:

> *Surely, he has borne our infirmities and carried our diseases; yet we accounted him stricken, struck down by God, and afflicted. But he was wounded for our transgressions, crushed for our iniquities; upon him was the punishment that made us whole, and by his bruises we are healed.*

The truth of the Lord bearing our diseases was made real for Israelites as recorded in Matthew 8:16-17 (NKJV):

> *When evening had come, they brought to Him many who were demon-possessed. And He cast out the spirits with a word and healed ALL who were sick, that it might be fulfilled which was spoken by Isaiah the prophet saying: He Himself took our infirmities and bore our sicknesses'.*

> **NIV:** *He took up our infirmities and carried our diseases.*

Healing all manner of diseases

So, while on earth in the days of his flesh the Lord not only healed *'all manner of diseases'* but also at times healed all sick that came unto Him. What's more, He unequivocally said that all who believe on

Him would do the same. But we have still not fully addressed the issue of whether on the cross he was made sick as well as being made sin for us. The key scripture bearing on this is Isa. 53: 4-5 which we now quote at length:

> **KJV**: *Surely He hath borne our **griefs** and carried our sorrows, yet we did esteem Him stricken, smitten of God and afflicted. Yet He was wounded for our transgressions, He was bruised for our iniquities, the chastisement of our peace was upon Him, and with his stripes we are healed.*

> **NIV**: *Surely He took up our **infirmities** and carried our sorrows, yet we considered Him stricken by God, smitten by Him, and afflicted. But He was pierced for our transgressions, He was crushed for our iniquities; the punishment that brought us peace was upon Him, and **by his wounds we are healed.***

> **The Amplified Bible:** *Surely He has borne our **griefs (sicknesses, weaknesses and diseases**) and carried our sorrows and pains (of punishment); yet we (ignorantly) considered Him stricken, smitten and afflicted by God (as if with leprosy). But He was wounded for our transgression, He was bruised for our guilt and iniquities; the chastisement (needful to obtain peace) and well-being for us was upon Him and with the stripes (that wounded) Him we are **healed and made whole**.*

> **New American Standard Bible:** *However, it was our **sicknesses** that He Himself bore, and our **pains** that He carried; yet we ourselves assumed that He had been afflicted, struck down by God, and humiliated. But He was pierced for our offenses, He was crushed for our wrongdoings; the punishment for our **well-being** was laid upon Him, and by His wounds we are healed.*

CEV: *He was wounded and crushed because of our sins; by taking our punishment, He made us completely well.*

NRSV: *Surely he has borne our infirmities and carried our diseases; yet we accounted him stricken, struck down by God, and afflicted. But he was wounded for our transgressions, crushed for our iniquities; upon him was the punishment that made us whole, and by his bruises we are healed.*

Points to note:

1) Clearly, several Bible translations have our Lord bearing **sicknesses** not just **grief**. There is argument about whether Isa. 53:4 refers to '**griefs**', as in the KJV translation, or to '**sicknesses**' (NASB and AMP) and '**infirmities**' (NIV). Since '**griefs**' mean much the same as '**sorrows**' secondary use of the word would seem superfluous in the KJV version. Actually, the Hebrew word translated '**griefs**' in the KJV is *choliy* (Strong's 2483) meaning 'malady, anxiety, calamity - disease, grief'. By contrast, '**sorrows**', (*makowb* in Hebrew, Strong's 4341) means both grief and sorrow, leaving *choliy* better translated as '**sicknesses**'.

2) Actually, in Isa. 53, Messiah is three times said to have been '**sick**'. Apart from verse 4, verse 3 also uses *choliy* to say He was 'a man of sorrows and acquainted with '**grief**' (i.e., **sickness**). And in verse 10 we are told '...the Lord hath put Him to **grief**'. Here again, '**grief**' is translated from a Hebrew word ***challah*** (Strong's 2470) which means to be sick and afflicted. So, the Lord was indeed made sick for us.

3) Then in verse 5 we read that the '***chastisement*** *of our peace was upon Him'* (NKJV). Chastisement in Hebrew is ***macrowth*** (Strong's 4149) meaning corrective punishment. Deut. 8:5

teaches '... *that as a man chasteneth his son, so the Lord you God chastens you*'. The question is, is disease this chastisement? From both the Old Testament and the New the answer is, **yes**. Deut. 28:21-22 lists the plague and other diseases which were to come upon Israelites for failing to obey God's commandments. And in the New Testament we learn in 1 Cor. 11:29-30 that failure to *'rightly discern the Lord's body'* (i.e., trust in the wonder of his blood shed for us and the whole life healing that comes through his flesh torn for us) resulted in weakness and sickness among believers. Paul goes on to say (verse 32) that *'when we are judged we are chastened by the Lord'*. The remedy then is to realise and believe that the Lord took both our sin and sickness upon Himself on the cross that we might be spared the consequences of chastisement and suffering for both.

4) In passing, note Israel's awful mistake when they saw Jesus on the cross. Far from seeing Messiah bearing their sin and sickness on their behalf they saw only a man who, they thought, had falsely claimed to be the Messiah and God, and was now being 'rightly' punished by God for doing so. If they saw Him made sick on the cross, it was, in their view, no less than He deserved.

5) The crux of the matter is whether Jesus was made sick with all of humanity's diseases on the cross, just as He was made to be *'sin for us who knew no sin'* or not? The above scriptures certainly show that He suffered our sicknesses and Isa. 53:10 says '...*Jehovah hath put Him to grief*' (ASV) and in a margin note gives the alternative reading: '(Jehovah) ... **made** *Him sick*'.

Why are some healed and others not?

Now, as to why some are healed and many are not, I suggest that the reason lies, as Paul intimates in 1 Cor. 11: 28-32, in the failure of believers to fully appropriate by faith all the benefits of the remission of sin and reconciliation with God effected by Jesus on the cross. I would also assert the balance of scripture teaches that it was to give us **health** (rather than the need for sporadic miraculous healings as such) that Jesus was made sick for us and died on the cross.

The difference is important. I know saints who certainly believe they are *'healed by his stripes'* but in their long lives have not suffered serious disease. Other genuinely saved people have suffered serious illness, on and off throughout their lives. Now, of course, eventually we all die but my serious belief is that, rightly appropriated by faith, the promise of being *'healed by his stripes'* is best fulfilled in those who by trusting God live healthy lives in the meantime.

Such folk are not seen at healing meetings, save perhaps to pray for others, because (if you would accept it) they have already been healed. As Jesus said, only *'they that are sick need a physician'*. Yet many Christians suffer disease in dreadful forms from stroke and paralysis through to cancer. And some suffer in this way for years. Is there a reason why?

I believe there is. Speaking in 1 Cor. 11:20-30 the Apostle Paul shares an important revelation about what happens when believers partake of the Lord's Supper *'unworthily'*. Evidently, some at Corinth were treating the bread and cup commemorating the Lord's death as an ordinary meal, thus profaning it. Paul rebukes them for eating before others could and for getting drunk.

Worse, treating the emblems of the Lord's passion with such disrespect was failure to *'discern the Lord's body'* (1 Cor. 11:29). Those who did so became *'guilty of the body and the blood of the Lord'*.

Even more seriously, Paul states: *'Because of this many among you are weak and infirm and some have died'* 1 Cor. 11: 30 (Interlinear Bible).

He adds that, in treating as commonplace the body and blood of the Lord, a man is *'eating and drinking judgement unto himself.'* And that judgement comes in the form of sickness and death. To avoid such dire punishment, he teaches, believers should;

1. Discern the Lord's body.
2. Discern, or examine themselves, for *'if we would judge ourselves we would not be judged',* 1 Cor. 11: 31.

The truth is that Jesus' blood is the holiest thing in all creation. It is the very life of God given to us and for us. His blood forgives, frees from sin, justifies us and heals our diseases. By his blood we can enter the very presence of God. Consequently, it is desperately dangerous to treat it lightly. Dishonouring the blood can make you sick, even cost you your life. In light of this Heb. 10:28-29 recalls that he who despised Moses' law died without mercy and asks:

> *'…of how much sorer punishment, suppose ye, shall he be thought worthy, who hath trodden underfoot the Son of God and hath counted the blood of the covenant wherewith he was sanctified an unholy thing and hath done despite unto the Spirit of grace'.*

Can I suggest one way to dishonour the Lord's body is to fail to believe that through his flesh his holy life is imparted to us? His body is the '*bread*' we should eat in faith and in no way can the Lord's body (his flesh) now be said to be sick. And surely it is dishonouring the Lord's blood if we discount all that it can do for us who believe. In particular that it is his blood that both makes us righteous, fully redeems us and gives us life and health. After all, scripture insists that our Lord saves to the *'uttermost'* those who trust Him. Meaning that

He wholly saves (or 'preserves') '*blameless*' our entire spirit, soul and body (1 Thess. 5: 23).

Furthermore, The Lord, speaking through the Apostle Paul, asserts in Rom. 8:10-11 that although *'the body is **dead** because of sin...*

> *...yet the spirit is **alive** because of righteousness' and that 'He who raised Christ Jesus from the dead will also give life to your mortal bodies through his Spirit who indwells you'.*

Without question, the cause of sickness is sin. Yet, as believers, we are *'made'* the righteousness of Christ' (1 Cor. 1:30). We have been justified and redeemed and if we walk in the light *'as He is in the light...the blood of Jesus cleanses us from all sin'* (1 John 1:7).

For all the above reasons it is no surprise that in John 3:1-2 the Apostle prays:

> *Beloved, I pray that in all respects you may prosper and be in good health, just as your soul prospers.'* (NASB)

A last thought: If Jesus now in heaven is not sick, nor the spirits of saints that are with Him, then why should we be, since, though presently on earth, *'... we are members of his body, of his flesh and of his bones'* (Eph. 5:30) and thus are united with Him?

Chapter Eighteen - IS JESUS JUST A MAN?

What is it with this 'Jesus is just a man' business? We seem to be hearing it strongly now. Bad enough that two or three decades ago the notorious 'Jesus Seminar' blackballed most of our Lord's gospel sayings in the Bible as spurious and denied both his miracles and those of his apostles. According to the 'Seminar', the historical Jesus was only a Jewish teacher, not God the Son, He did not have a miraculous birth, did not raise people from the dead, did not die for our sins, nor did He rise again.

But today even some of the best-selling supposedly Christian authors are putting out that Jesus was not the God of the Old Testament, had no existence prior to his birth from Mary, and though resurrected and exalted after his death, is still but a man and not the *'one true God'* (John 17:3) as such even today.

And, sadly, the argument that Jesus was but a man specially sent by God only at his baptism (not before) and that he had no prior existence to his birth is now becoming the default belief of many. Indeed, the divinity of Christ is now so under attack that it has become a major *'wind of doctrine'* (Eph. 4:14) tossing believers about left, right and centre and, in my view, undermining the faith of many.

And the argument being put forth is persuasive. Scriptures are presented that at face value appear to teach that the Father alone is the only true God and that the real Jesus Christ is the historic figure of a peasant prophet who lived in the Roman province of Judea nearly 2,000 years ago.

It is admitted by some of these revisionists that as the *'Son of man'* he was sent by God from his baptism onward, lived a life that pleased God – the only human being to do so – and died so that his blood could atone for our sins. But in all that he remained a man, the teaching goes. Though He is called the *'Son of God'* this does not mean He is God Himself, it is said.

A doyen of this 'Jesus is just a man' school of thought is historian Bart Ehrman, professor of religious studies at the University of North Carolina. He is author of several very popular books about early Christianity including *Misquoting Jesus* and *Jesus Interrupted.* His latest book is *How Jesus Became God: The Exaltation of a Jewish Preacher from Galilee.*

Ehrman claims that if Jesus had not been 'fictitiously' declared God by his followers Christianity would have remained 'just a sect within Judaism, a small Jewish sect'. He asserts that based on Matthew, Mark and Luke, Jesus in his lifetime didn't call Himself God, didn't consider Himself God and that his disciples had 'no inkling at all' that He was God.

Only in John's gospel, he argues, are found such statements as *'Before Abraham was, I AM'*, *'I and the Father are one'* and, *'If you've seen Me, you've seen the Father.'* His conclusion, apparently shared by many scholars now, is that the Apostle John's understanding of Jesus is 'not historically accurate'. In other words, the scripturally based belief that Jesus Christ is *'the first and last'* (Rev. 1: 11), meaning that He was God, is God and always will be God, is 'a myth'.

Supposed 'historical accuracy' has become the watchword for most of today's *avant-garde* writers and commentators on the Bible and Christianity. They include Ehrman, Anthony Buzzard, Greg Double, Marcus Borg and others. Almost without exception they either cast doubt on or limit the deity of Christ. Indeed, most deny him any pre-existence before his human birth.

And it seems the reason they do so is that they take a scholastic 'historical' approach to Jesus and the scriptures. What this means, as Ehrman puts it, is that 'historians, whether they are believers or non-believers, simply cannot say Jesus was raised from the dead because that would be to acknowledge that miracles are a true part of history when from a historian's point of view, they are not'. Deemed the most popular writer on the Christian religion in the world today, Ehrman reluctantly admits miracles may have happened in the past but insists 'they're not part of history'.

Notably, Ehrman says he was once a young evangelical Christian 'wanting to know how God became a man'. However, after concluding that the 'real historical Jesus' is not accurately recorded in the New Testament he is now an agnostic and, as a historian, wants to know 'how a man became a God'.

Denying the miracles

Even prominent authors who are believers are influenced by his academic, historical approach. For example, professor of comparative religion Marcus Borg deems miracles in the gospels 'metaphorical examples' not actual events while Unitarians such as Sir Anthony Buzzard and Greg Double believe that Christ had no existence prior to his birth from Mary.

This despite scriptures such as John 6:58-62 where Jesus challenges the *'many'* disciples who cannot accept Him as the *'bread come down from heaven'* (vs. 58), saying: *'What and if ye shall see the Son of man ascend up where He was before?'* (vs. 62). And what about John 17:5: *'And now Father, glorify Me with thine own self with that I had with Thee before the world was'*?

Greg Deuble seeks to explain away the plain meaning of this passage by saying Jesus didn't mean He had been in heaven with God in the past but was saying (prophetically) that He would be with Him in future, thus using the Hebrew prophetic penchant for saying something had already occurred (because it is in the plan of God) when actually it had yet to happen).

Granted, this idiom is sometimes employed by the Old Testament prophets but it is rarely used by Jesus in the New Testament. Actually, by not taking Jesus' words literally Deuble ignores the first rule of hermeneutics which is to take a non-enigmatic statement as it is read unless the context or mistranslation requires otherwise. Neither stricture applies to these verses as presented in the King James Version.

But in any case, why seek to change the meaning of Jesus' repeated statements that he came from the Father, was with the Father before the world began, came from heaven and would go back there? Answer: So that that only God (the Father) can be seen as God and Jesus can be demoted to be just a man. Thus the 'monotheism' of the Old Testament (*'Hear O Israel, the Lord our God is one Lord'*, Deut. 6:4, Mark 12:29) can be used to deny the commonly-held 'orthodox' position that God is a three-in-one 'trinity'.

However, the question of how God can have a Son when He remains the *'one true God'* is not resolved by denying clear scriptural statements that the Lord Jesus Christ is divine. There is another answer other than Tritheism - God in three separate persons - or Unitarianism which maintains that Jesus was just a man.

That God is One is undeniable. Jesus clearly says so (Mark 12:29). And Jesus upheld this 'Oneness' when he said: *'I and my Father and are one'*. Note that the word '*my*' is in italics, indicating that it is not in the original Greek. Therefore, what Jesus actually said was: *'I and Father are one'*. He also said He was in Father and Father in Him.

Beside Me there is no Saviour

You see, there is more than one way by which God can be One. The Unitarian approach is to deny the deity of Jesus Christ despite many verses which hail Him as God. For example, Thomas worshipped Him as *'My Lord and my God'* (John 20:28) and in Heb. 1:8 it is said of the Son: *'Thy throne O God is forever and ever'* and in vs. 10 it is said: *'And Thou, O Lord in the beginning hast laid the foundation of the earth and the heavens are the work of thy hands'*.

The other way out of the dilemma is to recognise that Christ Himself is God in all his fullness. That He is now the Father and the Spirit and Himself in One.

To me, the heart of the issue for a believer is: Who saved you and did He do it supernaturally or just as a man? Allow me to also ask: Do you experience the life of Christ in your heart? Do you rejoice at the difference **knowing** Him (not just intellectually but experientially, really and spiritually) makes in your life? Then ask yourself does this 'eternal life' that you are experiencing come from God or man? I would contend that it is the pre-incarnation Christ Himself speaking as both the Father and the Son when He says in Isa. 43: 11 and 1:

> *I even I am the Lord and beside Me there is no Saviour…*
> *I am the Lord your Holy One, the creator of Israel, your King.*

Agreed, there cannot be two gods or two saviours, only one. Most certainly God is 'One' and as the Lord Himself said there is only *'one true God'*. Who is He? My conviction is that He is the Lord Jesus Christ *'who was and is and is to come, the Almighty'*, as He said Himself in Rev. 1:8. In Him *'dwelleth the fullness of the Godhead bodily'* (Col. 2:9).

Against this view Unitarians such as Deuble and Sir Anthony Buzzard hold that Jesus never was God in the past, was only a man in his earthly ministry and though now in heaven is still only a man and not God Almighty despite his having been given *'all power in heaven and earth'* (Matt. 28:18) and been given a name – the *'Head'* – which is above every name (see Col. 2:19 and Phil. 2:9-11).

Against that I assert that Jesus Christ is the Creator of all things (Col. 1:15-19) and that He is also the creator of the new creation (Col. 2:10). As such He has *'the pre-eminence'* since in Him dwells all the fullness of the Godhead (Col. 1:18-19). And if this be so, how can it be said He is not God?

Chapter Nineteen - PASSPORT TO GLORY

> *Col. 1:27*
>
> *To whom (his saints) God would make known what is the riches of the glory of this mystery among the Gentiles, which is Christ in you the hope of glory.*
>
> **NLT:** *For it has pleased God to tell his people that the riches and glory of Christ are for you Gentiles too. For this is the secret: Christ lives in you, and this is your assurance that you will share in his glory.*

Fixing to fly abroad anytime soon? To do so you'll likely need two passports, one from your country of origin; the other to prove you have been Covid-19 vaccinated. What's more you'll probably need a certificate showing you have tested negative for the dreaded lurgy.

And it's much the same for believers whose hope is set on going to be with Christ in glory when they die. Not only will they need tangible proof they have been saved from the contagion of sin but also, they must have the 'passport' that is the Spirit of Christ within. Also, we must pass the test for holiness so that the Lord can present us *'faultless before the presence of his glory'* (Jude 24).

Problem is many have little or no idea of what really awaits them after death. The notion that a believer is whisked straight to consciously abide in heaven for ever still persists although there is not a single Bible verse to support it. True, Enoch *'was not, for God took him'* (Gen. 5:24) and Elijah soared into the sky aboard a chariot (2 Kings 2:11) but nowhere are present-day believers promised a similar direct ticket to live consciously in heaven in all eternity.

Nor is there validity in the 'beam me up Scotty' idea of going to heaven in the so-called 'rapture'. That word 'heaven' is not found in 1 Thess. 4:17, nor is there mention there of anyone going there in the verse. Rather, it describes how, in a distant time and in very different world, the dead in Jesus (and the transformed living) will rise to meet Christ in the skies then accompany Him back down to earth at his *'coming'* (Greek: *parousia*) when He returns to put down rebellion and punish unbelievers.

Serious Bible study suggests believers won't go to live consciously in heaven as their forever home for two reasons:

1) Positionally and spiritually, as grace-saved believers, we are already there, placed in spiritual authority with, and in Christ, who is *'far above all principality and power'*, in that we are *'seated in heavenly places in Christ Jesus'* (Eph. 2:6).

2) Secondly, because our real destiny, the purpose for which we are being saved, is to be resurrected to live on earth to rule and reign with Christ in his kingdom. That will be in the *'day of Christ'*, the centuries-long display of his power and glory from his throne above that long precedes his personal, physical coming to earth to reign in the Millennium.

The good news, and *'our blessed hope'* (Titus 2:13), is that we are bound for glory, his glory which will fill the earth during his day, *'the day of Christ'*. As the Lord Himself says in Num. 14:21, *'But as truly as I live, all the earth shall be filled with the glory of the Lord...'* Again in Hab. 2:13-14 He says: *'For the earth will be filled with the knowledge of the glory of the Lord as the waters cover the sea'* (And it will be glory such as has never been seen on earth thus far.

Importantly, it is the glory of Christ as God Almighty powerfully blazed forth so that all the world can see it).

For, although seemingly much of the professing church has forgotten about it, God's enduring and ultimate purpose is to save the world. The Samaritans said: *'…we know that this is indeed the Christ, the Saviour of the world'* (John 4:42). Jesus Himself said: *'God sent his Son into the world not to condemn it but to save it'* (John 3:17 and 1 John 4:14). However, as of now the Lord has yet to do so.

My conviction is that He will do so through his Holy Spirit by lavishing his love on people for centuries, while lifting every curse and restoring the earth to its pre-Flood pristine beauty in this wonderful epoch which scripture calls the *'day of Christ'*.

A foretaste of the glory to come

Meanwhile, let's explore how you and I can have a foretaste of this 'glory to come' in our life right now. This comes to us in three ways.

> First through the Spirit. After all God has not only promised us this but has already delivered it to us in the Person of the Spirit of Christ who lives within us.
>
> Secondly, through the Apostle Paul, He has told us to be *'looking for his appearing'* (Titus 2:13) and this **appearing** must take place to some extent in our lifetime for we will not need to be looking for it when we are already with Him in the life to come.
>
> Third, through the revelation of his truth the Lord has promised those who truly seek Him that they will be *'taught by Jesus'* (Eph. 4:20-21).

Sadly, very few are looking for his **appearing** today because they believe this will only occur at the end of the tribulation at the onset of the *'day of the Lord'*. I would submit the **appearing** comes much earlier as a glorious display of God's love and blessing for all mankind at the end of this present dispensation of the grace of God (Eph. 3: 2).

In the *'kingdom'* age that ensues, earthly fulfilment of prophecy resumes in force. Thus, we read: *'And the glory of the LORD shall be revealed, and all flesh shall see it together: for the mouth of the LORD hath spoken it'* (Isa.40:5*)*. And the Lord's appearing is a fulfilment of this promise.

In this marvellous day, the *'day of Christ'*, curses will be lifted, the light of truth shone forth, the earth restored to its pre-Flood beauty and mankind will be freed from sin, sickness, war and poverty, Meantime, please contrast this great time of blessing and love, the very next thing on God's agenda for the world, with the anger at wicked rebellion the Lord Jesus will vent at his coming in the *'day of the Lord'*. Which would you prefer: The Lord **appearing** in love, blessing and restoration or **coming** in fierce retribution in the *'day of the Lord'?*

Remember, the Apostle Paul promised believers of his day *'...rest with us when the Lord Jesus shall be revealed from heaven with his mighty angels in flaming fire taking vengeance on them that know not God and obey not the gospel of our Lord Jesus Christ, who shall be punished with everlasting destruction from the presence of the Lord, and from the glory of his power ... '* (2 Thess. 17-9).

Allow me to ask again: why are so many looking for the Lord's personal, physical return when He will bring destruction upon the world as the very next event on God's calendar? Why are they ignoring the blessing He will shine forth at his appearing at the dawning of the day of Christ, truly the next thing on the Lord's agenda?

Chapter Twenty -
SO WHAT SHOULD WE DO?

Six times in Paul's epistles in most Bibles, seven in the KJV, the Apostle presents the *'day of Christ'* as an imminent move of God and the very next thing believers should expect to see in their lifetimes.

Indeed, if I understand him aright, the Apostle Paul clearly implies that eagerly looking for this great event is vital to our receiving our full and final salvation. Accordingly, this chapter looks at what we, as believers, should do in the light of the truth of the *'day of Christ'* as taught in the seven Pauline references to this great new day.

The first mention is in 1 Cor. 1:6-8 and is foundational:

> *Even as the testimony concerning Jesus Christ was confirmed in you, so that you are not lacking in any gift,, awaiting eagerly the* **revelation** *of our Lord Jesus Christ, who shall confirm you to the end, blameless in the* **day of our Lord Jesus Christ** *(NASB).*

> *There is no single gift you lack, while you* **wait expectantly** *for our Lord Jesus Christ to* **reveal** *Himself. He will keep you firm to the end, without reproach on the* **Day of our Lord Jesus Christ** *(New English Bible).*

> *God thus confirming our testimony about Christ among you. Therefore, you do not lack any spiritual gift as you eagerly wait for our Lord Jesus Christ to be* **revealed***. He will also keep you firm to the end, so that you will be blameless on the day of our Lord Jesus Christ (NIV).*

*Even as the testimony of Christ was confirmed in you, so that ye come behind in no gift; waiting for the **revelation** of our Lord Jesus Christ who shall also confirm you unto the end, that ye be unreprovable in the day of our Lord Jesus Christ (ASV).*

These translations clearly show that it is the **revelation** of Jesus Christ in his day, the *'day of Christ'* that saints were to eagerly await and look for. For, in that day they would be found *'unreprovable', 'blameless'* and *'without reproach'* (Col.1:22). No mention here of anyone going to heaven or being caught up in the so-called 'rapture'. Rather, the believer is urged to look for the revelation or manifestation of Christ.

How then did this *'day of Christ'* come to be seen as something occurring at the Lord's return, his *parousia?* Answer: Because some translators have allowed their own theory of end time events to override and replace what the Bible actually says. Thus, in the King James Version verse 7 reads:

*So that ye come behind in no gift, waiting for the **coming** of our Lord Jesus Christ.*

But there is no *'coming'* in the original text. The Greek word, mistranslated *'coming'* in the KVJ is actually *apokulapsis*, meaning 'the appearing' or 'revelation' of Christ. His return to usher in the *'day of the Lord'* is not in view here but the revealing of our Lord to us, in our lifetimes, definitely is.

A further example of distorting the meaning is found in the Amplified Bible which adds Christ's 'return' to 1 Cor. 1:6-8 when no such word or meaning is found in the Greek. Thus, the AMP reads:

*... as you eagerly wait [with confident trust] for the revelation of our Lord Jesus Christ [when He **returns**]. And He will also confirm you to the end [keeping you strong and free of any accusation, so that you will be] blameless and*

*beyond reproach in the day [**of the return**] of our Lord Jesus Christ.* (AMP)

But again, there is nothing in the Greek New Testament text to support such addition to God's word, the meaning of which has been so corrupted in the process that today it is hard to find a single Christian who believes they should be looking for Christ's unveiling of Himself to them personally in their lifetime as the very next thing God will do.

That said, let's examine what *'waiting'* means in verse 7. The short story is that it means 'looking for with eager expectation'. The Greek word is *apekdechomai*, meaning to eagerly expect. 'Waiting' is far too weak a rendering of the real meaning which is to actively and eagerly, even to the point of groaning, look for Christ's unveiling in glory.

Just as Christ said, *'Seek ye first the kingdom of God and his righteousness'* before worrying where the next meal is coming from, so believers should also be looking for the revelation of Christ heralding the *'day of Christ'* as of more importance than anything else.

The serious Bible student might want to look up the translation of *apekdechomai* in the following verses where it is connected to *apokalupsis* 'the unveiling', for they speak of the wonderful revelation of Christ God wants us to see:

For example, Rom. 8:18-19 in the NASB says:

> *For I consider the sufferings of this present time are not worthy to be compared with the glory that is to be **revealed** to us. For the **anxious longing** of the creation **waits eagerly** for the **revealing** of the sons of God.*

Here 'revealed' is *apokalupto* and 'revealing' is *apokalupsis*. 'Earnest expectation' is *apokaradokia* meaning 'intense expectation' and 'manifestation' is *apokalupsis* yet again.

Again, this is a reference to the unveiling of Christ in the fullness of his glory in the *'day of Christ'* when He will shine forth not only as Himself but also to and in us who believe and now suffer for his sake. Why is it ignored in the common misunderstanding of what God will do next?

Rom. 8:23 and 25 further explain how we are to wait, look for and earnestly expect Christ's revelation of Himself, his 'appearing' and the shining forth of his glory. Verse 23 says: *'... we groan within ourselves waiting* (that is, looking eagerly) *for our adoption as sons, the redemption of our body'* (NASB). That's some serious looking folks.

> Verse 25: *But if we hope for what we do not see with **perseverance** we wait eagerly for it.*

And, of course, in 1 Cor. 1:7 *apekdechomai* is translated *'... awaiting eagerly the revelation* (apokalupsis) *of our Lord Jesus Christ.*

Gal. 5:5 states: *For we through the Spirit wait* (apekdechomai) *for the hope of righteousness by faith.*

Prosdechomai is translated *'looking'* in Titus 2:13 but means much more than casual observation. According to Strong's, the full meaning is to admit, i.e., the truth of, and through endurance to await its fulfilment with patience.

Phil. 3:20 - *For our citizenship is in heaven from which also we eagerly await [and look for] (apekdechomai) a Saviour, the Lord Jesus Christ.*

Heb. 9:28 - *So, Christ, having been once offered to bear the sins of many, shall appear the second time without sin to those that look for Him for salvation' (Interlinear Bible).*

In 2 Tim. 4:8 some Bible translations put off Christ's **appearing** into the far future. However, in the KJV and the ASV the word is 'henceforth', meaning that will occur from this time onwards. The New English Bible (NEB) rightly grasps the imminence of the event:

> *And **now** the prize awaits me, the garland of righteousness which the Lord, the all-just Judge, will award me on that great day; and it is not for me alone, but for all who have set their heart on his coming Appearance.*

So, what can we do but join the throng of those who look with irrepressible longing for the revealing of Christ in glory and we with Him? And we must look for this within our lifetime because it is only at his **appearing** we will be finally and fully saved. Furthermore, his a**ppearing** must occur in our lifetime here below because it will not be necessary to look for Him once we are with Him.

Thus, of Simeon (Luke 2:25-29) it is said he was *'waiting'* (looking for) the consolation of Israel … and it had been revealed to him by the Holy Spirit that he should not see death before he had seen the Lord's Christ. Having seen the baby Jesus he blessed God and said:

> *Now Lord, Thou dost let thy bondservant depart in peace, according to thy word. For my eyes have seen thy salvation.* (NASB)

My earnest prayer that each and every one of us who truly trust in the Lord Jesus may see Him appear for our salvation before we die and thus enter with Him into glory. But clearly, this will only happen if we are truly looking for his *'appearing'* and the *'day of Christ'* as our first priority.

APPENDIX -
SATAN'S GREAT TIME HOAX

The devil is not only the 'Great Pretender' – i.e., purporting to be God when he is not – he is also the 'Great Usurper' and the 'Great Pre-emptor'. That is, he anticipates what the Lord will do and presents his own counterfeit version first before God brings on the real thing.

The Apostle Paul said he was *'not ignorant of Satan's devices'* (2 Cor. 2:11) but sadly today many Christians are unaware of Satan's 'get in first' strategy and misunderstand scripture as a consequence.

For example, most fail to realise the devil, in the form of the serpent, was already in the Garden of Eden before God placed Adam in it (compare Gen. 1:25, 2:8 and 3:1). And he also 'got in first' by saying Adam and Eve would be *'as gods'* if they ate the forbidden fruit. This long before the Lord revealed the true way for man to be like God - that is, to be recreated in his image through the death, burial, resurrection, ascension and glorification of the Lord Jesus Christ.

The devil's pre-emptive strike

Satan made a further pre-emptive strike before Israel entered the Promised Land. Thus, even before God told Abraham He would give him *'this land'*, *'the Canaanite was then* (already) *in the land'* (Gen. 12:7). Now, as emissaries of the devil, Canaanites stand as the foremost of the *'serpent's seed'* (Gen. 3:15). They were descendants of the hybrid giants spawned when *'angels came in unto the daughters of men'* (Gen. 6:1-4). They were Satan's shock troops sent in to secure the Promised Land before Israel, the people of God, got to occupy it.

You see Satan always sends in the counterfeit first. That is why Jesus gave solemn warning to his disciples that this is what would happen during the *'day of Christ'* (Phil. 1:6, 10, 2:16), the pre-millennial kingdom of God in which He will rule over earth from heaven, saying:

> *Take heed no man deceive you. For many shall come in my name, saying I am Christ, and shall deceive many.* (Matt. 24:5)

Why do you need to know this? Because failure to take into account Satanic pre-emption warps our understanding of both the Bible and God's plan for the ages. In terms of what God will do next, believers require this information to be able to answer the important question of **when**.

In particular we now look at the great prophecies recorded in the Book of Daniel, for here the devil has pulled off one the greatest hoaxes in history. In fact, it would not be going too far to say that Satan has deliberately altered and re-arranged the course of history to cover up the truth of what these prophecies mean.

Allow me to explain. Most bible-reading believers know God gave King Nebuchadnezzar a dream in which he saw an image depicting five great world empires (Dan. 2:24-45). Now, it is commonly taught that this *'great image'* depicts four real empires of history with a fifth yet to come. They are seen as historical Babylon (a.k.a. the *'head of gold'*), historical Medo-Persia *('breast and arms of silver')*, the Greece of history (*'belly and thighs of brass'*, or bronze) and the historical Roman Empire *('legs of iron')* with 'restored' Rome yet to come (as the *'feet of clay and iron'*).

But and it's a big but, these empires of history cannot be the empires of Daniel's prophecy. For one thing, even today, none of them as described in Nebuchadnezzar's dream have come into existence as yet. Surely not, you say. Doesn't history record that the empires of

APPENDIX – SATAN'S GREAT TIME HOAX

Babylon, Persia, Greece and Rome really did exist in the past? Yes, it does, but the prophecies in Daniel are not about the past but the future; in fact, about a different age, a different world to be brought about by God thousands of years after Daniel's day and still to come after ours. And this timing is plainly set forth in scripture:

> Dan. 8:23 - ... *in the **latter time** of their kingdom when the transgressors are come to the full ...*
>
> Dan. 11:40 - *And **at the time of the end** shall the king of the south push at him...*
>
> Dan. 12:1 - *And **at that time** shall Michael stand up, the great prince which standeth for the **children** (i.e., later descendants) of thy people...*
>
> Dan. 12:4 - *But thou, O Daniel, shut up the words and seal the book, even to the **time of the end.***
>
> Dan. 12:9 - *And he said, go thy way Daniel: for the words are closed up and sealed **till the time of the end.***

Today, we are still not living *'in the time of the end,'* as many assert, for the *'latter times'* have yet to begin, let alone end. Another reason is that Dan. 3:44 says:

> *And in the **days of these kings** shall the God of heaven shall set up a kingdom which shall never be destroyed: and the kingdom shall not be left to other people, but it shall break in pieces and consume all these kingdoms, and it shall stand for ever.*

Most certainly that hasn't happened yet. So clearly *'the days of these of these kings'* are yet to come. Why then, one might ask, do so many teachers understand them as having been already fulfilled? The answer is that they failed to carefully study what scripture actually says, and to *'rightly divide'* it (2 Tim. 2:15).

But there's more, and for this I am indebted to bible teacher, Tom Ballinger who spent years prayerfully examining and *'rightly dividing'* (2 Tim. 2:15) the Book of Daniel. He was stunned to find the empires in Nebuchadnezzar's dream will exist only in a time yet to come. Now granted, there really were the empires of Babylon, Persia, Greece and Rome in past history but they were not and are not what the prophecy is about.

Let me say again, the heart of Nebuchadnezzar's 'Great Image' dream is that the empires *'broken into pieces'* by an everlasting kingdom will only come into being in the *'latter days'*, that is, in the *'hereafter'*. This is made clear in Dan. 2:28b and 29, which state that God:

> *… maketh known to King Nebuchadnezzar what shall be in the* **latter days.** *As for thee, O king, thy thoughts came into thy mind upon thy bed, what should come to pass* **hereafter***, and He that revealeth secrets maketh known to thee what* **shall** *come to pass.*

Clearly then the empires shown in the vision of the *'great image'* belong to the future, not the past. Thus, while Nebuchadnezzar truly was ruler of Babylon the world's greatest empire at the time he dreamed, the Babylon he saw in the *'great image'* vision lay far in the future. Indeed, it has not come into existence even in our day. It will only emerge in the coming *'day of Christ'*.

The four great empires still future?

The same can be said for the subsequent empires of silver, brass, iron, iron and clay (Medo-Persia, Greece, Rome and the latter-day empire of iron and clay, as the popular view of Daniel has it). Yes, such empires did indeed exist in the past but they did not fulfil the *'great image'* prophecy, for the simple reason that in their days 'God did **not** set up a kingdom which '*shall never be destroyed*' (Dan. 2:44). Therefore, they are still future.

But God **will** set up such a kingdom in the day of Christ after the five great empires portrayed in the dream prophecy hold sway successively over the earth in the first centuries of this wonderful new age now shortly to come to pass. Thus, again your attention is drawn to importance of **when.**

You see, diligent bible study shows that both the **latter days** (Dan. 10:14) and **hereafter** (Dan. 2:28b and 29, 10:45) refer to the period mentioned as '*the last day*' in the gospels and later designated by the Apostle Peter as the '*times of restitution of all things*' (Acts 3:21). This special day of God's dealings with man is termed the '*day of Christ*' (Phil. 1:6, 10 and 16) by the Apostle Paul. It is when Christ will shine forth his glory from heaven at his '*appearing and his kingdom*' (Titus 2:13, 2 Tim. 4:1). It is when the Lord will inaugurate his rule from heaven over earth. It is when He will '*judge the quick and the dead*' (2 Tim. 4:1).

So how come most bible interpreters have had it wrong all these years? Short answer: the devil. He has so engineered world history, to make it 'his story', that he has fooled nearly all of God's people into believing the bulk of Daniel's prophecies have been fulfilled already. In effect he has persuaded them that he, the devil, is fulfilling Daniel's vision, not God, and that, indeed, he has already done so.

But, you say, is the devil able to contrive and bring about in real life his version of history, and make the whole world run to his programme? Well, yes, he is. Didn't the Apostle John write: '*The whole world lies in the power of wickedness*' (1 John 5:19)? Didn't Paul the Apostle say '*... the course of this world (is) according to the prince of the power of the air, the spirit that now worketh in the children of disobedience*' (Eph. 2:2)?

When Jesus was tempted in the wilderness Satan declared that he, not God, held power over all the kingdoms of the world and offered them to the Lord if only He would worship him. What's more Jesus did not argue against his claim or deny that Satan held such authority (Luke 4:5-7).

So, then, hard as it may be to believe, Satan has engineered and brought about four great world empires thousands of years ahead of the time God said they should exist. Why? To obscure and hide the truth of the *'latter days'*, the *'day of Christ'* in which such empires will flourish under his (Christ's) rule, not just their own.

You see, in God's plan of the ages, the four yet-to-be raised up Gentile world empires, as depicted in Nebuchadnezzar's dream, will hold sway for some 700 years in the coming *'day of Christ'*. This timing is deduced from the Dan. 9: 24-27 'seventy weeks' prophecy.

But, I hear you say, wasn't the 'seventy weeks' prophecy largely fulfilled at Christ's first coming? Well, no, not if you see it from God's perspective. And, again, as He sees it, the fact that the empires of Babylon, Medo-Persia, Greece and Rome did rule in ancient times does not fulfil the prophecy of the 'great image' dream.

Again, allow me to explain. The reality from God's perspective is always his rule and the execution of his plan and purpose for the ages. This will stand regardless of whatever in the meantime, to human eyes, seems to totally contradict it.

God's end game

Now, at the time of the dream Nebuchadnezzar's Babylonian empire held sway over the earth. Sadly, Israel, which should have been *'the head, not the tail'*, no longer existed as a nation in her own land. Conquered, killed and dispersed with only a few believers surviving in captivity the people of God were as far from being the vehicle to bring the God's rule on earth as it was possible to be. All because of their rebellion against the Lord and descent into idol worship, of course. Consequently, the devil, to all intents and purposes, now ruled the earth through the person of Nebuchadnezzar.

Yet God, looking far forward to the end game, saw something entirely different. He foresaw an earth ruled from heaven, a new age in which all men would bow the knee to his Son and every tongue confess the name of Jesus as the God who became man and, on dying for our sin, was exalted by God to bear a name above every name (Phil. 2: 9-11).

What's more, this future Lord of glory revealed Himself as such to Daniel at least twice during the prophet's lifetime. That is, He appeared in vision to Daniel as *'the great God and Saviour'* (Titus 2:13) and the *'blessed and only Potentate, the King of kings and Lord of lords'* (1 Tim. 6:15) He is and will be revealed as such to all men in the soon coming *'day of Christ'*, the next great event on God's calendar. Read about these visions in Dan. 10: 1 and 5-6:

> *In the third year of Cyrus king of Persia a thing was revealed unto Daniel, whose name was called Belteshazzar, and the thing* (i.e., message) *was true but the time appointed was long…*
>
> *Then I lifted up mine eyes and looked and, behold,* **a certain man** *clothed in linen, whose loins were girded with fine gold of Uphaz. His body was also like the beryl*[1] (a precious stone, sea-green in colour) *and his face as the appearance of lightning, and his eyes as lamps of fire, and his*

---

[1] The beryl appears in Rev. 21:20 as the eighth foundation of 'the new Jerusalem'. It signifies that the holy city's inhabitants will occupy it through resurrection.

> *arms and feet like in colour to polished brass, and the voice of his words like the voice of a multitude.*

Here the Lord appears in all his heavenly glory as He will *'at his appearing and his kingdom'* (2 Tim. 4:1) when He is made manifest to all men at the start of the *'day of Christ'*. In that day all on earth will know Him; they will bow the knee to Him who, though God, humbled Himself to become a man and die. They will bow the knee to Him and confess that He is Lord.

Daniel then, in this vision, was being carried far forward in time to see Jesus as He will be when He is revealed to all in heaven and earth as the Saviour and God of all men, as the *'judge of the quick and the dead'* (2 Tim. 4:1) and to Whom all will bow at *'his appearing and kingdom'*.

And what did the coming Lord of all (Phil. 2:9-10 and Eph. 1:20-22) tell Daniel about the time when He would be revealed in his glory? In Dan. 10:14 He said:

> *Now I am come to make thee understand what shall befall thy people in the* **latter days** *for the vision is for many days.*

Again, in Dan. 7:13, 10:9-19 and 8:15-19 Daniel is fast forwarded in time to see the Lord in glory *'as one like the Son of man'*, to see Him approach *'the throne of the Ancient of Days'* and to be spoken to and even touched by Him.

At the time of the end

Furthermore, it seems all the heavenly visions imparted to Daniel in his book concern or culminate in the *'***latter days***'*, a.k.a. the *'day of Christ'*. For example, in Dan. 8:17 and 19 the angel Gabriel tells Daniel:

APPENDIX – SATAN'S GREAT TIME HOAX

> *Understand, O son of man: for at **the time of the end** shall be the vision. And he said, Behold I will make thee know what shall be in the last end of the indignation, for at the time appointed the end shall be.*

The words *'at the time of the end'* and their equivalents run like a river through Daniel's prophecies. Thus in Dan. 10:1 Daniel understands that *'the thing was true but **time appointed** was **long**'*; After being foretold of the rise and fall of Persia and of Greece the prophet is reminded by the angel in 11:27, '*for yet **the end** shall be at **the time appointed**'.*

As to Daniel's own people, he is told that even those that *'understand'* shall fall (11:35) *'to try them and to purge, and to make them white, **even to the time of the end: because it is yet for a time appointed**'.*

The *'latter days'* timeline is restated again in 11:40 - *'And at **the time of the end** shall the king of the south push at him* (until the indignation be accomplished) *and the king of the north shall come at him …'*

Thankfully, for Israel there will be deliverance amid her great trouble in these times. Dan. 12:1 proclaims that:

> **At that time** *shall Michael stand up, the great prince which standeth for the children of thy people, and there shall be a **time of trouble** such as never was since there was a nation, even **to that same time**, and **at that time** they people shall be delivered, every one that shall be written in the book.*
>
> *And many of them that sleep in the dust of the earth shall awake, some to everlasting life and some to shame and everlasting contempt. And they that be wise shall shine as the brightness of the firmament: and they that turn many to righteousness as the stars for ever and ever.*

We Gentiles should not be ignorant of these *'latter days'* for the resurrection that occurs then will at the start include us. Accordingly, in 2 Tim. 4:1 the Apostle Paul tells Timothy:

> *I charge thee before God and the Lord Jesus Christ (who) shall judge the quick and the dead at his appearing and his kingdom.*

This kingdom, of course, is the Lord's *'heavenly kingdom'* (2 Tim. 4:18), to which we Gentile, grace-saved saints of the *'high calling'* are summoned. It is the time when the Lord will rule from heaven over earth, as we see Him doing, in rehearsal, as it were, in the Book of Daniel.

To sum up, we learn again that asking the question '**when**?' reveals huge and important truths. Among them is that the devil hijacks human history in a bid to forestall God's plan and determined eternal purpose to fully redeem mankind. However, he will not succeed. God is actually the Lord of time and his purpose will be accomplished perfectly, no matter if it takes thousands of years.

So, both Israel and we Gentiles, look for our resurrection in the **latter days**, the *'day of Christ'* which He inaugurates through his *'appearing'* (Titus 2:13). It is both our *'blessed hope'* and theirs. Let us look for it and lay hold of it now.

APPENDIX -
TIMING – THE SECRET OF THE KINGDOM PARABLES

Matt. 13 - *Behold **a sower went forth to sow**. And when he sowed, some seed fell the wayside and the fowls came and devoured them up.*

Luke 8:8 - *And other **fell on good ground** and sprang up and bear fruit an hundredfold. And when He had said these things He cried, he that hath ears to hear let him hear.*

Ps. 126:6 - *He that goeth forth and weepeth bearing **precious seed** shall doubtless come again with rejoicing bringing his sheaves with him.*

Eccl. 11:6 - *In the morning **sow thy seed** and in the evening withhold not thine hand for thou knowest not whether shall prosper, this or that, or whether they shall both be alike good.*

Isa. 55:10-11 - *For as the rain cometh down and the snow from heaven and returneth not thither but watereth the earth and maketh it bring forth and bud that it may give **seed to the sower and bread to the eater.** So shall **my word** be that goeth forth out of my mouth and shall not return unto Me void, but it shall accomplish that which I please and it shall prosper.*

Amos 9:13 - *Behold the days come, sayeth the Lord, that the plowman shall overtake the reaper, and the treader of*

> *grapes him that **soweth seed** and the mountains shall drop sweet wine and all the hills shall melt.*

There is much more to the kingdom parables of Jesus than that which meets the eye or ear. However, it takes but a glance at the gospel narrative to see they bear one message to the crowd and quite another to the chosen disciples. Beyond both these messages, however, lies an even deeper meaning that has to do with God's unfolding of his plan for the ages and the role of the called and chosen within it. And that is the subject of this study.

Let us begin by looking at the parable of the sower and Jesus' explanation of it (Matt. 13: 3-9, 18-23 and Luke 8: 4-15). This parable is often seen as a picture of how Israelites really sowed seed in Jesus' day, but it is not. No sower worth his salt would sow seed in stony ground, plant it among thorns or try to get it to grow on the trodden down footpath.

Rather, he would carefully plough and till a selected plot or field, removing the stones and thorns until it became 'good ground' and only then sow his seed. Why? Because seed corn is costly. In hard years farmers went hungry and their children sometimes went without bread to preserve enough seed to sow their fields again.

To this day seed corn costs far more to buy than ordinarily harvested grain. This is because it has to be specially dried, treated and preserved to ensure it will germinate when sown. It is indeed *'precious seed'* (Ps. 126:6). Similarly, *'the word of truth, the gospel of your salvation'* (Eph. 1: 13) is precious, having been carefully preserved in your Bible.

Naturally speaking, no farmer, whether in Jesus' time in Israel or now, who was in his right mind, would sow precious seed willy-nilly, as the sower in the parable did. **But God would.** God would sow randomly because God sows by grace through faith and is not willing that any should perish. Accordingly, He freely scatters the precious seed of his word, his gospel, among all people, even those with the hardest, stoniest hearts.

The Israelites of Jesus' day then, were meant to grasp from this parable that the 'sower' was not a man but God Himself. What's more they should have realised from the way Jesus was telling the story that He was the Messiah and was now present among them. However, spiritually speaking, Jesus Himself is the 'seed' (Gal. 3:16) that is sown. Those *'with ears to hear'* (Matt 13: 9) then would realise He was the seed that had come to them in a season of the Father's *'sowing'*.

The point of the parable is that the outcome of his visitation with them - whether there was a harvest of sufficient souls to save the nation - would depend on how the Seed was received, whether in good ground or bad. This is why no 'harvest' features in this parable - only the sowing and growing.

Luke 8:11 specifically says the *'seed'* is the *'word of God'*. Yet in Matt. 13: 19 it is *'the word of the kingdom'*. Why the difference? Answer: Jesus at first was *'sent only to the lost sheep of the house of Israel'* (Matt. 15:24), and thus the good news of the kingdom was properly first and foremost to the chosen nation. Later, however, there was an 'overspill' of the word to others, even to Gentiles.

Are only few saved?

This is why the Apostle Peter tells a largely Roman, that is, Gentile, audience in the house of Cornelius (Acts 10: 36-38) that *'that word, I say, ye know'*. Earlier, in sharp contrast, he had told an entirely Jewish crowd in Jerusalem at Pentecost, *'For the promise is unto you, and to your children, and all that are afar off...'* meaning only Israelites (Acts 2:39). Thus, we see that in the Acts period the sphere of the preaching of the gospel of the kingdom was widened by way of application from Israelites to others.

Well, so much for the message to the crowd. What was the meaning to the disciples? Privately Jesus tells them that the parable of the sower explains why *'only few'* are saved. It is because the devil makes the receiving of the seed unfruitful in many people's hearts. Thus in Matt. 13:19 He says:

> *When anyone heareth the word of the kingdom and understandeth it not, then cometh the wicked one and catcheth away that which was in his heart. This is he which received seed by the wayside.* (KJV)

To the disciples then, the parable, as explained by Jesus, told how the devil sought to thwart the preaching of the kingdom gospel at every stage by snatching away the word, preventing hearers from understanding it, stopping others from becoming *'rooted* in Christ (Eph. 3:17, Col.2:7) and swamping those who at first received the word with either the *'riches'*, or the *'cares'* of this world.

Against such poor returns from the hard, stony or thorn-choked soil, the *'good ground'*, according to the parable, brought forth *'some an hundredfold, some sixty and some thirty'*. Yet the disciples saw little evidence of such marvellous growth and harvesting in the three and a half years of Jesus's ministry nor in their own subsequent ministry in the Book of Acts. At best the return was meagre as a little math shows. If each of the twelve apostles and 70 disciples saw only 12 souls saved in their personal ministry, one each for the 12 tribes of Israel, then the number saved would have been 98,400. But there is no evidence in the Book of Acts such a figure was ever reached.

What's more, if each of the 12 souls saved under the preaching of each apostle/disciple had brought forth a 30-fold increase in fruitfulness by witnessing to others, then the total saved would have been nearly three million, about the population of Judea at the time. Clearly no such large-scale conversion took place.

Why so? The answer is that the time for the great harvest had not come in the time of Jesus and his disciples. It did not come in the Acts period, nor has it come in ours. But it will come.

You see, the parable of the sower is timeless, in that it does not designate when the seed was sown, nor when it will be harvested. Certainly, it could be applied to the preaching of the kingdom of heaven in Jesus's time and subsequently in the Acts period. But actually the *'word'* of the kingdom had been proclaimed long before. For example, in Gen. 1:26 God said, *'Let them (mankind) have dominion ... over all the earth'*. And dominion means 'kingdom'.

Thy kingdom come

The 'word of the kingdom' was proclaimed again in Dan. 7:13-14 when it was prophesied:

> *One like the Son of man ... came to the Ancient of Days ... and there was given Him dominion, and glory, and a kingdom, that all people, nations, and languages should serve Him: his dominion is an everlasting dominion, which shall not pass away...*

The question is, of course, when will such kingdom and glory happen? When will the Son of man and his chosen ones have dominion over all people? The answer is, when the seed of the word of the kingdom *'brings forth an hundredfold'*. And when will that be? It could, of course, have been in Jesus' time, for the kingdom of heaven was then *'at hand'* (Matt. 4:17). But it wasn't. Again, it could have come in the Acts period had Israel then repented of crucifying her Messiah and received Him as King. As the Apostle Peter told the Jews in Acts 3:19-20 - *'Repent ye therefore ... and He shall send Jesus Christ which was before preached unto you.'* But it didn't.

When therefore would *'thy kingdom come'*, as our Lord told his disciples to pray for (Matt. 6:9)? Answer: not yet. And that it would come 'but not yet', was the deeper, hidden meaning to not only the parable of the sower but also to the other kingdom parables Jesus told.

This is borne out by the timeline interpretation of the parable of the sower as given in App. 140 of *The Companion Bible*. This suggested agenda sees:

The first sowing *'by the wayside'* as the kingdom proclamation by John the Baptist, who, like Jesus said, *'Repent ye, for the kingdom of heaven is at hand'* (Matt. 31-2, Mark 1:1-8, Luke 3:1-18, John 1:6-36). In this *'sowing'* the opposition of the evil one is seen in the birds of ill omen (as also in the parable of the 'mustard tree' (Matt. 13:30-31). The seed was *'devoured'* and the word *'not understood'*.

The second sowing was by Christ Himself (Matt. 4:17), then by the Twelve (Matt. 10:7) and the Seventy (Luke 10:1-20). This sowing was *'on stony ground'*. It was received at first 'with joy' (Matt. 13:20, Mark 6:2, 12:13 and Luke 4:22) but became unfruitful for lack of root (Mark 4:16-17).

The third sowing was by Peter and the Eleven and 'them that heard Him' in the Acts period (Heb. 2:3). It was *'among the thorns'*. Peter proclaimed the kingdom (Acts 3:18:26) and repeated the call to national repentance, still the abiding condition for national blessing. But the seed was choked. Thus the *'thousands of Jews'* who at first 'received the word', became *'all zealous of the law'*, rather than Christ and the kingdom (Acts 21:20, Gal. 1:3-5, 10-13; 4:9; 5:1-4). This sowing came to a crisis in Acts 28 when the kingdom was ultimately rejected and has been in abeyance since.

The fourth sowing is in the future. It is the *'holy seed'* that is to be sown after long desolation in answer to the prophet's cry *'how*

APPENDIX – THE SECRET OF THE KINGDOM PARABLES

long?' (Isa. 6:11-13). My belief is that it will occur during the centuries-long display of Christ in his kingdom glory in the *'day of Christ':*

> *And in that day shall the deaf hear the words of the book and the eyes of the blind shall see out of obscurity; and out of darkness.* (Isa. 29:18)

In Matt. 24:14 the Lord specifically stated that the **gospel of the kingdom** would be preached in all the world as a witness to all nations; *'and then the end shall come'.* Is it being proclaimed in the all the world today? Is it being 'preached to every creature' (Mark 16:15) now? The answer is, no. Today it is the *'the grace of God which bringeth salvation'* and that *'hath appeared unto all men'* (Titus 2:12) that is being preached. Today God is manifesting Himself through the word (of grace) largely committed unto Paul the Apostle and written down by him in his epistles (Titus 1:3).

And Titus 2:12-13 makes plain that this gospel of the grace of God is teaching us that right now we should, *'live soberly, righteously and godly, looking for that blessed hope, and the glorious appearing of the great God and our Saviour Jesus Christ'.*

This is why in 2 Tim. 4:1 the Apostle Paul speaks of the Lord Jesus Christ *'who shall judge the quick and the dead at his appearing and his kingdom'.* Now, it should be obvious that this kingdom cannot come unless first the good news of its coming is first preached worldwide.

This successful harvest proclamation, with a one hundredfold return, I submit, will occur at Christ's appearing to usher in the *'day of Christ'.* It is then that the light of the glory of Christ will blaze forth upon all men. It is then that the deaf will hear the good news of his kingdom; it is then that the eyes of the blind shall see out of darkness to perceive the truth of the heavenly Saviour and King.

It is then, for the first time in history, that the seed sown will fall into good ground and bring forth fruit *'some an hundredfold, some sixtyfold and some thirtyfold'*.

APPENDIX -
THE SEED THAT GROWS BY ITSELF

Jesus' parables about the kingdom mention the seed sown but only one mentions the harvest. That is the story of the seed that grows by itself in Mark 4: 26-29. Like other parables this one explains what the kingdom is *'like'*. But, unlike the parable of the sower and that of the wheat and tares, no further explanation of what it means is given by Jesus.

Instead, it is left to us to understand it as best we can and for that we need the help of the Holy Spirit. Under his guidance I see important differences. The sower in Mark 4:26-29 is but a man and a somewhat ignorant one at that. In the parable of the Wheat and Tares the sower is *'the Son of man'* (Matt. 13:37) but in Mark 4:26-29 the sower, having sown, goes his way and sleeps. What's more, He *'knoweth not how'* the seed of the kingdom sprouts and grows. That can't be said of the Lord who never sleeps and who created heaven and earth, nor of the Jesus who when on earth displayed an intimate knowledge of seed growing in both this and other parables.

However, it is not natural seed that is in focus here but the *'word of the kingdom'*. You see, prior to his resurrection and ascension Jesus Himself did not know just when the gospel of the kingdom would be brought to a full harvest to save the world. So, when asked by the disciples, *'Will you at this time restore the kingdom to Israel'* (Acts 1:6), He replied: *'It is not for you to know times and epochs which the Father has fixed by his own authority'* (NASB). And in Matt. 24:36 He said:

> But of that day and hour knoweth no man, no, not the angels in heaven, but my Father only.

In sharp contrast today the risen glorified Lord Jesus Christ has *'abounded unto us in all wisdom and prudence',* even making known to us *'the mystery of his will'* (Eph. 1:8-9).

So then, in the parable of the seed that sows itself Jesus could not set out a precise timetable for the kingdom of God to come but He could describe the process. And that process was, and is, that the kingdom will come in stages:

> *For the earth yields crops by itself: first the blade, then the ear, after that the full grain in the head. But when the grain ripens, immediately He puts in the sickle.* (Mark 4: 28-29)

The *'blade'* then, in this understanding, is the impact Jesus' preaching of the kingdom, demonstrated as it was by stunning miracles, had in his three-and-a-half-year ministry on earth. Thousands of Israelites believed and were saved.

The next stage of plant growth, the *'ear'*, describes the wider and greater impact that miracles accompanying the preaching of gospel of the kingdom had in the Acts period. Importantly, it was at this time the good news of the kingdom, the much better world to come, was spread to the Gentiles. Note that both the Lord's actual ministry on earth and that through the apostles in the Acts period occurred during the *'day'*. In John 9:4 Jesus told his disciples:

> *We must work the works of Him who sent Me as long as it is day; night is coming when no man can work.*

In the Mark 4:26-29 parable we are told the kingdom is…

> *…as if a man should sleep by* **night** *and rise by* **day**, *and seed should sprout and grow, he himself does not know how.*

I suggest that *'night'* came when the huge outburst of spectacular miracles largely stopped at the end of Acts, though some persist even today. This *'night'* has prevailed up to the present time. It is an epoch *'where no man can work'* the outstanding miracles Jesus and his apostles did, though they may well see lesser ones. Today no-one holds meetings to walk on water or to raise the buried dead. But the miracles of being saved, of knowing heaven in your heart, seeing Christ by vision, knowing his presence and hearing his voice are available to every believer.

If the *'ear'* period of kingdom growth halted nearly 2,000 years ago at the end of the Book of Acts when does the *'full grain in the ear'* appear? The answer, according to Jesus, is that *'immediately'* He sees the grain is ripened, He *'puts the sickle in'* and the *'harvest is come'* (see Rev. 14:15).

My conviction is that the harvest is imminent now. No special prophecies have to be fulfilled for it to take place. The only proviso is that we believers are looking for it (Titus 2:13) because already the fields are *'white unto harvest'*.

www.ingramcontent.com/pod-product-compliance
Lightning Source LLC
Chambersburg PA
CBHW072340300426
44109CB00043B/1974